BUDDHA'S BOOK
of MEDITATION

JEREMY P. TARCHER / PENGUIN
a member of Penguin Group (USA)
New York

BUDDHA'S BOOK
of MEDITATION

Mindfulness Practices for a Quieter Mind,
Self-Awareness, and Healthy Living

JOSEPH EMET

JEREMY P. TARCHER/PENGUIN
Published by the Penguin Group
Penguin Group (USA) LLC
375 Hudson Street
New York, New York 10014

USA · Canada · UK · Ireland · Australia
New Zealand · India · South Africa · China

A Penguin Random House Company

ISBN 978-1-62953-543-2

Printed in the United States of America

Book design by Lauren Kolm

NOTES TO THE READER

There are many reasons for taking up the practice of meditation.

There are also many ways of practicing mindfulness.

I learned many of these from Thich Nhat Hanh, my teacher, who is the inspiration behind this book, and discovered others through my own practice.

These many reasons and many ways are explored at length in this book.

Self-regulation, better relationships, and developing a compassionate heart are significant benefits of meditation; here, they are given the importance that they deserve.

We recognize now that the role of the brain in guiding our life has its downside as well as its many benefits. I use the word *brainfulness* to describe an attitude of unexamined bondage to the biases and priorities of this organ, and suggest that mindfulness is an effective counterweight to it.

Practice material is integrated into every chapter—and to make practice sessions more enjoyable, many of the exercises are songs that you can download and use as "mindfulness mantras" to inspire and guide your practice. This material is available at Mindfulness MeditationCentre.org under Buddha's Book of Meditation.

The message of this book is empowering; whether you would like to be more positive, more peaceful, less anxious, or angry less often, you can change in ways that you desire.

The brain is plaster, you are the sculptor, and mindfulness meditation is the tool. It is my fervent wish that this book will be useful to meditation students and teachers and to those in the helping professions who want to use meditation with their clients.

—JOSEPH EMET

There is no enlightenment outside of daily life.

—THICH NHAT HANH

CONTENTS

* Audio accompaniment for the Guided Meditations and Practice Songs is available for download at MindfulnessMeditationCentre.org under Buddha's Book of Meditation.

FOREWORD

When we sit in meditation, we follow our breath, and we are aware of our feelings and states of mind. When we stand up and walk, when we eat, have a cup of tea, or talk with someone, we continue to be mindful in the same way. For a practitioner, there is no line that separates meditation from everyday life, or everyday life from meditation.

We can all take a few conscious breaths and let go of impatience, hurry, or stress as we go through our day. Living mindfully makes it possible to be in the present and to transform our lives into a work of art where each moment reflects the beauty, wisdom, and love that we all have in our hearts.

Joseph Emet's book describes how we can apply mindfulness to different areas of our life, and how doing so can enrich the way we live. When we shine the light of mindfulness onto all aspects of our lives, we have a chance to live happier and more fulfilling lives as free persons.

The practices in this book include many songs as well as guided meditations, poems, and meditation themes—elements that are also part of our practice at Plum Village. May it be of help in moving your practice forward.

—THICH NHAT HANH
Plum Village, France

INTRODUCTION

*People seem not to see that their
opinion of the world is also a
confession of character.*

—RALPH WALDO EMERSON

The scenery around me this evening is the most beautiful I have ever seen, be-cause it is *now*. The choppy waters of Lake St. Louis are licking the rocks just below where I sit in real time, and not on a replay of a memory reel. Unlike remembered suns, the sun of now warms me to the core, and the seagull overhead calls with this moment's voice. I am fully present as I take in this scene with all my senses.

Why should one meditate?

Because the world is a beautiful place, and we miss its beauty when we are not "there."

Because we are humans with huge brains and compelling thoughts. Our thinking often takes us away from the moment.

Because coming to our senses requires a bit of practice—"Just do it" does not always work, just as it would not work if somebody handed you a guitar and said, "Just play it."

Meditation is the formal practice that leads to the ability of using the brain instead of being used by it.

In twenty years of teaching mindfulness meditation, I have seen people come for many reasons, including the search for better sleep, better relationships, more creativity, calming the overthinking mind, reducing stress, becoming less anxious, and controlling anger. Just as learning to play the guitar enables us to play sad songs, happy songs, or love songs, learning meditation techniques helps us to guide the brain in directions that we want.

In a meditation class of mine, Karen confessed to me: "I am overwhelmed by my emotions about my boyfriend. His needs take up all the space in my life. I want to meditate because I need to make time for myself. I need to learn how to manage my emotions better."

Wallace came because his marriage was on its last legs. He had a habit of zoning out every time his wife started speaking. She wanted him to be more present, but this seemed to be beyond him at the moment.

Like many others, Karen and Wallace found help in mindfulness meditation.

They learned general mindfulness practices as well as specific contextual hints about how to apply them to their personal concerns. In this book, you will find these same general techniques as well as help with particular issues that may concern you more intimately. The premise of this book is that meditation affects every aspect of life—when your stress level goes down, all aspects of your life are improved, and when you live a more inspired life, all areas of your life benefit.

We are not stuck for life with our present stress level or our present anxiety level. We are not stuck with our present way of relating to others, or the state of our moods. We are not stuck with our default feelings. All of these—as well as our present attitudes and mental habits—can be changed with mindfulness practice. Many people, from athletes to businesspeople, are already using mindfulness techniques to increase their effectiveness and success level. Many others are using them to improve the quality of their personal lives.

There are exercises within boxed text in every chapter, and they are clearly explained. They include guided meditations, meditation themes, and practice songs. They are recorded for you and are only a click away at mindfulnessmeditation centre.org. Mindfulness songs add variety and interest to meditation practice. If you listen to or sing a song often, it becomes an earworm. It hums practice basics in your ear and transports you to places you long to be in. As it grows on you, it helps you to grow as well. A song can be an effortless reminder and an inspiration to practice. My teacher Thich Nhat Hanh once referred to me as "a bodhisattva of music"—as I wrote some of the practice songs used in centers in his tradition around the world.

Download them and the guided meditations to your iPhone, computer, or favorite digital music player, and take them with you. Do you have to wait for someone? Is there a free moment at home? Just sit comfortably and use them to light up your mind and your day.

In my experience, each meditation period is different—each brings a new perspective or opens a new door. That is because the context of each meditation session is different—it is the changing panorama of my life. The basics are the same—calming the mind and opening to insight—but they are practiced on new ground every day. I kept this in mind as I wrote this book: each chapter is designed to bring a new perspective to your mindfulness practice or to your day. Start with the basics, but do not stop there. Take advantage of the richness of the mindfulness practices that are presented here. You are more likely to continue meditating if you can learn to make the practice contextual and relevant to the changing circumstances of each day.

The brain is just another organ, with its own biases, illnesses, humors, and tumors.

It helps to understand how this organ developed through evolution, and further chapters explore the link between Buddhist thought and evolutionary psychology.

Why are we the way we are? Why do we have so much anxiety and so much aggressiveness? Evolution sheds a light on this and provides another imperative for mindfulness practice—we do not want to be prisoners of our evolutionary heritage, Flintstones in our fast, shiny cars, living in a dream world somewhere between the vestiges of our wild past and the realities of our sobering present. Specific practices address this issue.

We will start this journey with the need to listen to the voice of our brain with a grain of salt. This practice has been at the forefront of psychotherapy lately, but as you will see in the next chapter, it is equally important for everyone—it is necessary for leading a happy and positive life.

1

ARE YOU BRAINFUL OR MINDFUL?

> *Nonviolence, which is a quality*
> *of the heart, cannot come by an*
> *appeal to the brain.*
>
> —MAHATMA GANDHI

We are "brainful" until we realize it. Then we can become mindful, at least momentarily, because our frame of reference is now larger.

Our brains are constantly telling us things in the form of automatic thoughts, ruminations, emotional thinking, cravings, fears, or impatience. That is what automatic thoughts are—the brain doing a monologue. We get a "brainful" of this all day long.

We stay "brainful" when we say "Amen" to everything our brain tells us.

Meditation is keeping an eye on the brain.

We become mindful when we become nonjudgmental observers of this monologue—we become observers of our human nature.

"But we are all human," you might say. "Of course we possess human nature. What's wrong with human nature?"

Many things, as truth commissions in diverse places such as Argentina, South Africa, and Canada found out. Many things, as tobacco company trials discovered. Many things, as our news media reveal every day. Love, poetry, and altruism are part of human nature, but so are lying, cheating, violence, and murder.

The same brain that inspires us to love also sometimes whispers to us to cheat.

The same brain that makes us long for peace also incites us to start wars.

And the same brain that wants to care for the environment forgets all its concerns when its own convenience is at stake.

Our brain has particular biases. Here are some of them:

The negativity bias of the brain is well documented. Even a healthy brain has it—it makes us remember negative things and forget the positives. And, according to research, with time, our memory of a negative event can get even more negative. The brain makes us pay attention to negative stories—thus the litany of negative headlines in newspapers and on the evening news. The media people know that bad news is "good" news, and they want to keep our attention. They serve us what will do the job. They also provide us with an abundance of horror movies, dramas, thrillers, and murder novels.

The brain does not want us to sleep if there is perceived danger. Anxiety keeps us awake.

The brain is interested in survival and safety. When it takes over, it goes to unreasonable lengths that border on paranoia to fight for and ensure its safety and survival.

Food is one of its principal concerns regarding survival. The brain would rather err on the side of safety—it would rather we overeat and store food as fat than risk starving. For most of our history on Earth, humans and other animals evolved in a context of scarcity. The brain has not yet adjusted to a world of plenty. Animals eat competitively and often in a hurry—before someone else gets it.

"Fast food" has a long history.

Brains place a high value on reproduction. The male spider's brain pushes it to sacrifice its life in order to couple and transmit its seed. Male animals sometimes get killed in the battle to become the alpha male and inseminate the females in the herd.

And females reproduce in order to, well, reproduce.

It has been said that a deer does not have to run faster than the wolf in order to save its skin. It only has to run faster than one other deer. The brain's perspective on self-interest is narrow. Even ultrasocial insects like ants are only interested in the welfare of their own colonies. An animal does not worry about global warming or pollution.

Even laziness may have an evolutionary value.

In the wild, most animals face limited food supplies and thus have a finite amount of energy to spend. Evolution may have primed us to conserve energy and not move around unnecessarily. I recently saw a documentary on polar bears and watched a mother bear lumber around the ice sniffing the air for traces of prey. She hadn't eaten for eight months while continuing to nurse her cubs. Seasonal famine is a way of life for many animals—this bear was definitely not thinking about going for recreational swims or hikes. After checking out possible sources of food around her, she lazed around conserving energy. Her voice is inside us today, whispering things such as, "Don't walk to the corner store. Drive so you can conserve energy." I hear her voice when I drive to the gym; it says, "Park as close to the door as you can so you don't have to walk far." Funny, as I go there to exercise in the first place.

In a world of feast or famine, an individual needed to eat as much as she could in order to survive periods when food was scarce. Dogs, still remembering the irregular life of hunting packs, exhibit this tendency to compulsively overeat when given free access to food. Evolutionary laziness, when coupled with the evolutionary urge to overeat, becomes a deadly combination in our day.

Do you recognize familiar patterns here?

Without mindfulness, we repeat these patterns.

But isn't mindfulness itself a brain function?

Of course it is. But it is a metafunction. Here are some of the distinctions:

With "brainfulness," your brain is in charge.

With mindfulness, you are in charge.

Your TV set has no biases. It plays the channels you choose.

Your brain comes preprogrammed with biases—it is like a TV set that automatically goes to the food sites or the competitive sports sites when you turn it on. Some of its other general biases were listed earlier. You can discover others that are specific to your own brain in your meditation practice—perhaps your brain is prone to anger, perhaps to anxiety.

Without mindfulness, we end up watching the channels our brain chooses because of its biases.

The mind, on the other hand, can include our values—it can go beyond the built-in biases of our brains. It can also include wisdom. Mindfulness is paying attention intentionally. When we are mindful, we pay attention selectively and purposefully. We do not download all the brain blabber to the desktop of our consciousness. Aware that the negativity bias of the brain exaggerates negativity, we compensate for it by intentionally paying attention to the good and the beautiful. Aware that habits can be formed intentionally as well as unintentionally, we choose to go in the direction of our values by consciously creating beneficial habits through repetition. Aware of the preciousness of this moment, we intentionally savor it. We intentionally pay attention to our breath and to the signs of tension in our bodies so that stress does not accumulate during the day and become distress.

I use "brainfulness" to mean a state of total identification and fusion with the messages, urges, and compulsions coming from the brain. It is a state where the brain is mistaken for the self, and the two merge into each other. A "brainful" person assumes, "I am my brain," without articulating that thought as such, and identifies not only with the thinking capacity of her brain, but also with its emotional aspect and its many biases and evolutionary features.

This state of identification has been described in the context of psychotherapy, when a person's brain messages bring her grief. But *all* brains are like compulsive backseat drivers—they do not stop talking. Learning to listen to this talk with a grain of salt is not only important at the therapist's office—it is also important at the shopping center, at the dining table, and at work.

It is not *always* wrong to follow the brain's advice.

But it is usually better to do things out of wisdom.

MINDFUL LIVING

The price of healthy living is continual mindfulness.

The taste buds do not entirely forget their evolutionary cravings. If they did, the food industry would be happy to remind them. Frito-Lay did not invent the craving for salt. You can sometimes see deer licking salt by the side of mountain roads in the winter. Frito-Lay cashed in on an inborn tendency without stopping to think about whether they were doing us a favor.

Our popular culture has been formed by our brains without much wisdom.

Pop music, magazines, and TV ads are pushing us toward mindless living a good deal of the time.

Our most cherished values, such as honesty, integrity, and respect for life, often go directly against the interests of the brain. Living by our values is a good way of going from "brainfulness" toward mindfulness.

EMBODIED WISDOM

Do you remember the time when you were learning to drive?

The rules of traffic are pretty simple, but an intellectual knowledge of driving a car is different from the feeling you get when you slip behind the wheel. Now, your *body* needs to drive the car as well as your brain; your feet, your hands, your eyes, and your ears need to be coordinated with your thoughts. When you think *left turn*, your body must execute the maneuver smoothly.

Embodying peace is also quite an apprenticeship.

You can read about peace in a book by Thich Nhat Hanh in relatively short time.

But consistently embodying peace as you walk, eat, and do the dishes every day is another matter. And speaking peacefully, under provocation in an argument, under stress in front of a group, or when you feel anger takes a whole lot more than an intellectual understanding of peace.

Relax.

People spend eight weeks in a stress reduction course to teach that one word to their bodies. And some come back for a second session.

BRAIN ON A PEDESTAL

Thomas Edison said: "The chief function of the body is to carry the brain around." These words put the brain on a pedestal, or at least in a wheelbarrow. Let us balance it out with thoughts such as, "The chief function of the brain is to look after the survival and the well-being of the body." The relationship is not one-sided. To be a more beneficial partner, the brain has to give up some of its own interests and priorities. It (at least the male brain) may get lots of pleasure from driving very fast, but if it is oblivious to the interests of the body, it may end up in a crash, killing the body and thereby itself. It may get intellectual pleasure from playing computer games or solving theoretical problems while eating junk food and shortening the life of the body and its own life. It may enjoy designing more lethal nuclear weapons while shortening the life of our species on Earth.

Let us also add looking after the well-being of our environment as an important function of the brain, for without a healthy environment, we also get sick. Reread the preceding list of what brains are interested in. You can see how mindfulness differs from "brainfulness."

Going from "brainful" to mindful is like swimming upstream. Swimming upstream starts with intention and requires energy. Otherwise, we may drift toward the polluted waters of an unhealthy lifestyle while doing what our brain tells us to do.

THE RUNAWAY BRAIN

We are more than our brains, just as we are more than our stomachs or our sex organs. However, when I look at some very large people, it does look as if the stomach is running the show for them, and when I look at some sex-charged magazines it does look as if our sex organs are running our lives. That's easy to see, because we know what the stomach or the sex organs are interested in. We know very well in what directions they are pushing us to behave. Yet most of us manage to bring some balance into our lives. We manage to listen to other voices inside us and not just to the loud clamor we get from the stomach or the sex organs. That is because we recognize their voices. (If you are one of these people who have difficulty having a two-way conversation with your stomach, this book will help.)

We do not recognize the voice of the brain as such. We consider it as our own voice and identify with it even though, as an organ, the brain also has its own interests just as the stomach and the sex organs have theirs. The brain does not observe disclosure rules of its interests while it pushes us to behave in certain ways. Our brains carry the dreams and the nightmares of our evolutionary past, our negativity bias, the biases of our culture and gender. This issue is at the top of the agenda for psychotherapists now because the brains of people with mental challenges such as depression and anxiety are telling these people things that are making them sick. Hearing the voice of the brain without identifying with it has become an important therapeutic goal. But this is also an important growth goal for all of us. We do not want to be prisoners of the biases of our brains. We do not want these biases to limit or pollute our vision and our life.

MEDITATION AND THE RAT RACE

The brain is the organizer-in-chief of the rat race, because it evolved from rats (we share a large percent of our DNA with them) and other similar creatures.

It fills sports arenas with people who come to see men bash one another up just as they came to watch gladiators in Roman times. It makes us buy powerful new cars that can go amazingly fast even though the speed limits on our streets make this particular power useless.

We have *rat* in our genes, but we must also have *flower* in our genes somewhere, although further away in time.

That is where mindfulness comes in. *Flower* is further away in our consciousness, and its voice is fainter. That does not mean that it is less important.

Rat is closer to us in evolutionary time, and its voice is louder. That does not mean it is more important.

Without mindfulness, it is easy to *become* a rat. With mindfulness, it is *possible* to become a flower.

THE HOLISTIC VISION

Happy people live seven to ten years longer, and a holistic view is important for our happiness. All parts of the body and mind must be taken into consideration if the whole is to be happy. If you have any doubts, try going for a walk with an ill-fitting shoe that pinches just one toe.

Listening to one part of you to the exclusion of other parts creates imbalance, disharmony, and sickness. If you listen to the voice that says, "Eat, eat, and eat," then you may get so chunky that it may be difficult to have sex. You have made one part of you happy, but another part unhappy.

If, on the other hand, you listen to the part that says, "Have sex with all the attractive people you can find," you may find that your relationships and your family life go downhill—that is not a good recipe for happiness either.

If you listen to the voice of fear and prevent yourself from going forward, you may make a part of you temporarily happy but, ultimately, the fearful part is also part of the whole. And as the whole experiences stalling and boredom, it becomes unhappy as well.

In the short run, the squeaky wheel may get the oil. But in the long run, the other wheels need to be oiled as well, otherwise you may need road service—for what is required is not just the smooth functioning of one wheel, but the smooth running of the whole car.

The holistic view extends beyond the immediate self and encompasses community as well. People who do service work as volunteers report extended feelings of fulfillment and happiness.

No man is an island,
Entire of itself,
Every man is a piece of the continent,
A part of the main.

These words were written by the seventeenth-century poet John Donne in a poem appropriately titled "Meditation XVII." In our day, that feeling of community extends to the community of all beings and to the environment as well. The last lines of John Donne's poem sound strangely relevant today:

And therefore never send to know for whom the bell tolls;
It tolls for thee.

Through the practice of mindfulness we develop the skill of hearing the voices of the different parts of the self without identifying with any particular voice—without conferring the title of "I" to it. The brain message that says, "I'm bored," is no different from the stomach message that says, "I'm hungry." It is the voice of an organ in distress. The "I" in each case is not the whole of you—it is a part of you. It is an organ speaking. And it is through mindfulness that we develop the skill of listening nonjudgmentally to our internal voices. The brain often gives us contradictory messages: when you are angry with someone, one part of your brain might say, "I'd like you to wring his neck," while another part may say, "Oh, wait, that might be against the law." If you mistake a part for the whole and do its bidding, then the rest of you can suffer unpleasant consequences, such as spending time in jail. A map of the brain looks a little like a map of the European Union, with a similar disparity of voices and urges coming from different regions.

MINDFUL, FORGETFUL, BRAINFUL

Thich Nhat Hanh often uses *forgetful* as the opposite of *mindful*. Instead of being aware of the wonders of our beautiful Earth, of the miracle of being alive, and of the privilege of being human, a forgetful person glides through life in a haze of unawareness. She is not aware of her breath, her body, or her posture.

In this book, I'm suggesting *brainful* as another antonym of mindfulness, because I wish to draw attention to what is there instead of what is missing: a "brainful" person is most likely also forgetful, but the feature I wish to emphasize is that her mind is *full* of brain messages reflecting the biases and preoccupations of her brain. These messages could represent particular challenges such as anxiety or low self-esteem if she has them, but even in the absence of such particular challenges, her mind is still full of our built-in evolutionary concerns for survival and reproduction, media-culture messages about buying and consuming more or looking a certain way, or messages reflecting our negativity bias.

GUIDED MEDITATION
Listening

The quieter you become, the more you can hear.
—RAM DASS

Thinking is the mind talking.
Meditation is the mind listening.

As I put myself into the listening mode,
    my mind becomes quiet so it can hear.

First, I listen to my body.
When there is a sharp pain somewhere, my body talks loudly.
Now, it is talking quietly.

I have to listen carefully
    so I can hear the quiet messages coming from my body.

My body does not talk in words—my legs do not speak English.
My body talks in sensations.
If I hear words, it is the brain talking.

It is the brain interpreting or judging the sensations coming
from my body.

I listen to all the sensations of breathing.
They are nothing spectacular, but they put me in touch with
my body.
My body is expanding and contracting
as it takes in, and then expels air.

I'm interacting with the Earth as I breathe.
The Earth is not only rocks and dirt,
it is also water and air.

I could not live long without this interaction,
I live from breath to breath.
My life consists mainly of interacting with the Earth.

How do I listen now?
Do I listen with boredom or with interest?
Do I always listen like this?

When I hear my brain talking,
I say, "Shush, I'm listening."

I listen to each part of my body one by one.

I listen with particular attention for signs of tension.

When I find tension, in my hands, shoulders, neck, or abdomen,
    I let go and relax.

Now, I listen to my facial muscles:

They are closely coordinated with my thoughts.

I let go of tension in my forehead,
    and form a gentle smile around my eyes and mouth.

Contentment is a bodily feeling.

Now, I feel contentment in my body.

VISUALIZE THE BRAIN

We see arms and legs and eyes and ears all day long. We feel our heartbeat, and see hearts on Valentine's Day greeting cards and in children's storybooks. We feel our stomach, its hunger as well as its satiety, at least three times each day. In contrast, we do not see or feel our brains. We have "headaches," not "brainaches." We even learn multiplication tables "by heart."

The brain is an invisible organ. It is quiet—it does not beat like the heart, grumble or burp like the stomach, or cough like the lungs. It gets assimilated into the self. It is helpful to disentangle the two.

Visualize your brain—it is like soft tofu or Jell-O, and it is suspended in fluid. It is also quite delicate. Pinkish or light beige in color. Weighs about as much as a medium-sized coconut. Packed with neurons that create thoughts and mental pictures much as the hardware behind a television set creates images—now even 3-D images. Yes, images seem to be a different category of "thing" than wires, but nobody disputes that they are somehow created in the maze behind the TV screen. Unfortunately, for much of history, people had difficulty conceiving that the hardware of the brain could produce the software of thoughts and images, and the brain managed to evade responsibility for its actions. Its current behind-the-scenes role is partly the result of history.

Acknowledge the role and responsibility of your brain in driving your behavior, but also be aware that your behavior in turn drives the brain: the brain is plastic and changes physically according to the demands you make on it and how you feed it—how you eat.

2

SERENITY MEDITATION

You are the sky. Everything else—
it's just the weather.

—PEMA CHÖDRÖN

Buddha lived and meditated outdoors as a homeless seeker during the six years before his enlightenment, and also afterward. He meditated under trees, in the forest, and by streams. One particular tree that he sat under, the Banyan tree, is still there and is a place of pilgrimage for Buddhists. Banyan is a kind of fig that is now the national tree of the Republic of India.

Meditating outdoors puts us in natural surroundings—it also makes it easier to "come to our senses," as the outdoor air is alive—it is animated by the wind and caresses the skin as it moves around us. Other senses are also engaged: birds come and go, sing, or tweet. Leaves rustle. There is always some kind of smell in the forest—the smell of freshness, of rotting leaves, or the bouquet of flowers, and an endless variety of colors and shapes to gaze at lovingly when you open your eyes. There are no walls such as those that surround us when we are indoors, and that liberates the eye and, with it, the mind. Meditating outdoors is a special kind of joy—and once you taste it, you can bring the same feeling with you as you move your practice indoors.

Indoors, the nature inside us engages our attention: the body that pulses with the heartbeat, the abdomen that constantly changes shape like a balloon, our sitting posture that resembles a small mountain, our straight spine that is like a tree trunk, the sensitive skin that glows with sensations when all else is quiet, and, above all, the brain that is always trying to steal our focus. Like a child who is trying to get your attention and is waving her hands in your face, the brain is waving its self-important thoughts at you, and if you lose your concentration for one moment, you will find yourself in its tight embrace. Then you are gone—no longer meditating but floating unawares from thought to thought, until you realize what happened and come back home to the warm, pulsating body, to the breathing and shape-shifting abdomen, to your posture, to the living here-and-now.

Serene, like an image of the Buddha.

Do you sometimes wish you could be like that more often?

Buddha's serenity was earned—it was a result of his meditation practice. And it is not true that he was serene because not much was happening in his life. A serial killer once accosted him in the street, a mean relative dislodged a huge boulder on a cliff as he was passing under it, and once somebody sent a crazed elephant running wildly at him. He was serene under all those circumstances, and more. Not only was he serene while sitting in meditation, but sitting in meditation was how he attained serenity. In the following pages, I will take you through some essential steps toward serenity meditation that reflect my own experiences.

First a proviso, and some preliminaries. The proviso is that serenity meditation and insight meditation are usually taught together, as Buddha himself taught them, perhaps because as our minds become calmer, deeper layers of inspiration have a chance to surface and come to the fore. The converse is also true— as we get more insight into where our agitation comes from, we tend to be less reactive. But I will start with serenity here because it is important for so many people. As you go on with the rest of the book, you will get the full package.

Now to the preliminaries. If you are already familiar with these, please feel free to skip them, or read along for a refresher.

POSTURE

"Cross-legged" does not give a good description of the meditation posture. For many of us, "cross-legged" evokes a posture with a curved back. To get a description and pictures of a good meditation position, search for "Burmese meditation posture" on the web. The important feature of this is that there is a firm cushion under the buttocks, and the knees are on the floor. Do not worry too much about getting one heel over the other foot.

If the knees do not want to touch the floor, you have two choices:

1. Give them time. If the knees are in the air when you start, let them be. You will find that they will soon relax and get lower with time and gravity.
2. Raise your buttocks higher by getting a thicker or a harder cushion. This makes room for the knees. The important thing about a meditation cushion is its hardness. Good meditation cushions are filled with kapok or buckwheat shells, and they do not flatten out when you sit on them. You can also put an additional pillow or folded blanket on your meditation cushion to get extra height.

Attention to Posture Is Part of Meditation Practice

We meditate not only with the mind but also with the body. When attention wavers, good posture is one of the first things to go. Do not wait till you *feel* like sitting up. Sit up with good posture, and you will feel right. If you sit with a slouching posture, you will feel hazy. When the brain detects that the body is sitting with an erect, attentive posture, it produces the right feelings. Mindfulness meditation grounds us in the body and brings the mind and the body together. Attention to posture is part of that process, and a straight back is an important element of good posture.

There are two main reasons for sitting with a straight back:

1. When the whole spine is in alignment all the way up to the neck, you do not have to work hard to fight gravity. As many of us normally sit with a bit of a slouch, a straight back feels unnatural at first, but it is less tiring in the long run. Extra bonus: if you suffer from backaches, you may find that consistently sitting with a straight back for a few weeks makes the back less painful.
2. A straight back makes room for the breath. As we breathe from the abdomen, we put air in the tummy area. When we slouch, this area is compressed, and there is not as much room for the breath.

To compensate for a slouching habit, do two things:

1. Try the opposite of slouching. Arch your back and stick out the tummy as you sit. See how that feels. You do not need to continue sitting like that as you meditate, but that initial arching will counterbalance a natural slouch you may have and help you get to a straight back.

2. Reach back with your hands and feel the postural muscles on either side of the spine. Those should be taut. They hold you up. In contrast, the abdominals should be soft. They breathe.

MEDITATE TO FEEL ALIVE

In mindfulness one is not only restful and happy,
but also alert and awake.
—THICH NHAT HANH

There are therapies such as Hakomi that go into the meaning of posture and look into how our state of mind creates our posture, and vice versa. "This system of thought allows us to look at the body as an expression of mental life, which we do very deliberately and precisely, in the study of character, body structure, posture, and behavior," writes Ron Kurtz, the creator of Hakomi. You can have fun with this in front of a mirror: compare what you look like with a head-forward, slouching posture as opposed to a head-held-back, spine-straight posture. More important, notice how each posture *feels* in your body and mind.

A good meditation posture is neutral.

It is also open. Some Yoga teachers go into the meaning of the different energy centers of the body, known as the *chakras*. Notice that in the meditation posture, all the energy centers feel open. As you hold your head straight, the throat is open. As you hold your back straight, the heart and the abdomen centers are open. And the root center is also open. In the meditation posture, you do not feel "closed in" on yourself. And with a straight back, energy circulates freely in the body instead of feeling blocked.

Sit with your hands folded on your lap. When the hands touch, the two sides of your body come together. You can also feel your expanding and contracting abdomen inside your arms as you breathe.

The Eyes

Relax the eyes, and relax the eyelids—let them droop until they are almost closed. The eyes are our most important sense organ, and it helps to conserve the energy and attention that they normally absorb. We stop actively looking, focusing, or searching with the eyes. The eyes are passive—a little bit of light gets in and helps us to stay in the here-and-now. That is also what we do with the other senses— we cannot close off our skin, our ears, or our nose, but we can switch to being passive observers of our sensations.

Changing Your Attitude Toward Discomfort

If you want to stay in your comfort zone, you might not want to go out into the cold mountain air to ski. You might not want to put out the energy to go and exercise. You might spend a lot of time in bed. Our culture of indulgence does not serve us well when we want to do things that move us in the direction of our values.

Start appreciating the feel of the meditation posture as you already value the small discomfort of an exercise session or a Yoga class. "No pain, no gain" may sound a bit masochistic at first, but notice that just living involves some discomfort. Getting up in the morning, going to work, and undertaking some area of study or training all involve some discomfort. We would not avoid discomfort altogether even if we did not do these things. We would instead have the worse discomfort of having a mostly empty life. We know this and have generally come to terms with it—yet I notice that in each new class, someone would like meditation to be an exception to this rule. I sometimes get questions such as if one can meditate lying down. I keep waiting for a question about whether one can meditate while sipping a martini.

(This is not meant to discourage those who have a particular challenge that prevents them from sitting on the floor. In that case, use a straight-backed chair and sit straight with both feet flat on the floor.)

Energy and Motivation

Sometimes, part of our energy flows into channels that are dead ends, such as regretting the past. Other mental activities such as ruminating, obsessing, worrying, and overthinking are drainpipes—they just drain our energy away. Meditation conserves energy by checking these habits. It also puts us in touch with our true self and our values. This is a winning combination: sensing a build-up of energy, knowing where to spend it, and feeling inspired to do so.

EAT WELL TO MEDITATE WELL

Do not expect to find deep-fried foods, red meat, or alcohol if you go to a meditation retreat, or if you spend some time in a Buddhist center. You will notice that they choose what they put into their bodies with care: They eat healthy foods. This is not only for ethical concerns such as not killing animals but also because one can meditate with a clearer mind if one eats brain-healthy foods. It makes sense to eat a poor diet consisting of sugary drinks, junk foods, and oils that taste like they came from the crankcase of a car only if you believe that what you eat has nothing to do with the health of your brain, nothing to do with how you feel, and nothing to do with how long you are going to live. The effect of a poor diet on the brain is not visible, because the brain is tucked away in the skull. However, it is possible to see this effect with an MRI scan.

Physician and brain scientist Daniel Amen talks about "brain envy." As he describes it, brain envy happens when he shows a new patient who has not been eating and exercising well an MRI scan of her brain side by side with the scan of a healthy brain. He relates that the differences are so obvious that the effect is instantaneous: The patient resolves to eat better on the spot, because she wants to have a healthy brain like the one she just saw.

We can see the effect of what we eat on our bodies when we look in the mirror and examine our waistlines. We cannot see our brains in the mirror. We are likely to ascribe all the problems that come from a poorly nourished and poorly functioning brain to our upbringing or to the weather. These problems can range all the way from feeling foggy to anxiety and depression. Adequate amounts of vitamin D and fish oils are essential for brain health. In addition, some food-conscious people are now avoiding gluten, and you may like to take a look at Dr. David Perlmutter's book *Grain Brain* for the reasons. It turns out that, for many people, gluten creates inflammation in the body and the brain, especially now that agribusiness has created varieties of wheat that contain *forty times* more gluten than it did previously. Many of these new kinds of gluten are compounds with which our body is not familiar. Dr. Perlmutter, a neurologist, considers that gluten consumption may be a contributing factor in Alzheimer's disease and other dementias. He compares eating gluten to drinking gasoline.

FORMAL AND INFORMAL MEDITATION

Walking is a kind of meditation also. Henry David Thoreau walked for about four hours each day and said that if for some reason he was prevented from taking his walk, he did not write that day. In a broader sense, each moment of the day can be turned into a meditation if we approach it mindfully and with reverence. Yet for me, there is a special magic in sitting meditation. I enjoy walking and doing everyday activities in a meditative spirit also, but so far they do not replace a period of sitting meditation for me.

WHERE AND WHEN

Sometimes you meditate because you are in the right mood, and sometimes you get in the right mood because you meditate. If you wait for the right mood to come first, you may wait for a long time, and then forget. This is what happens to people who fail to keep up their meditation practice.

I took a poll in a recent workshop with advanced meditators and found that some of them just sat up and meditated in bed in the mornings. This was not the only time they meditated, but they found that it was a good way to dispel the morning fog and start the day with a clear mind.

Some others had a meditation cushion in their bedroom.

The Special Magic of Early Morning Meditation

A beneficial custom that comes from tradition is the practice of meditating early in the morning. In *Buddha's Book of Sleep*, I mentioned that many of us spontaneously wake up around three in the morning and stay awake for a while. That may be the origin of early morning practice—the conscious mind has just taken a good rest, and the basic stretch of deep sleep that we all need to survive is done. As our consciousness reboots, it sees things with a fresh eye. The mind is still in contact with the unconscious life force that has been running our body while we were sleeping, and we have one foot in each camp, as it were—our consciousness has just woken up, and the unconscious energy has not yet completely receded. This can be a creative moment, a moment to reenergize and refocus—a window opens to a different kind of understanding for a brief while, and if you are present to catch the occasion, you can get a glimpse into a new way of seeing things. If there is an outstanding issue or a question in your mind, you may well see it with different eyes after a period of morning meditation.

How Long

When you use the guided meditations in this book, they will serve as a timer as well. When you are doing silent meditation, I often recommend a short period of "warming up" first. The warm-up could be listening to or singing along with a practice song, or reading a poem or another appropriate short text. Thich Nhat Hanh's books are a gold mine of inspiration for bringing you to a meditative spirit.

If you have only five or ten minutes, however, just sit and go directly into following the breath. Bring your attention from the head region, where thoughts happen, down to the abdomen, where breath happens. Stay in touch with your breath during the whole time you have. You will find yourself energized and re-focused.

Allow yourself to sail into deeper waters at least once a week. If your meditation period is progressing well, take the time to go longer—about forty minutes is a good length if you want to go deeper in meditation. Thich Nhat Hanh compares this kind of sustained concentration to the sustained fire that makes it possible to cook potatoes or rice.

DEALING WITH THOUGHTS

One good way to deal with the abundance of thoughts is to begin labeling them as they occur. This requires a good deal of concentration, as thoughts have a way of slipping through the net with which you set out to catch them. Persevere, though—when people go fishing, they do not aim to catch every single fish that comes along. In the beginning, you may catch just a handful of thoughts at a time. Be happy with your catch, come back to the breath, and cast your net again.

However, many beginners do not experience individual thoughts—they feel a stream of thoughts, or they feel that they are struggling in a sea of thoughts. I was like that when I first started. I did not feel thoughts in a way that I could label them—I felt them like fish experience water; I imagine that fish do not experience water drop by drop. The challenge then is to pry oneself loose from the thought-space, to separate oneself from the grip of the mind-space. One way to do that is by directing the attention toward the body and the breath. Another way is to visualize climbing out of the river of thoughts to sit on the grassy riverbank, and to start watching the flowing river.

We have more than one river flowing inside us.

You can do the following exercise by watching the river of feelings, or by watching the river of thoughts. Sometimes the two even merge into one, such as when we experience a thought as an articulate kind of feeling.

MEDITATION THEME
Watching the River of Feelings

"In us, there is a river of feelings in which every drop of water is a different feeling, and each feeling relies on all the others for its existence. To observe it, we just sit on the bank of the river and identify each feeling as it surfaces, flows by, and disappears."

This quote from Thich Nhat Hanh's book *Peace Is Every Step* can serve as the theme for a meditation session. Visualize a flowing river. Perhaps you have already sat by a river and watched it flow. In that case, let that be the model for your visualization.

Your meditation cushion is a rock, a park bench, or the soft grass by that river.

Being aware of your breathing helps you shift into the observing mode.

Observe each drop, each feeling, nonjudgmentally—without either identifying with it or rejecting it.

There may be a leaf floating on the river. See it also as a feeling. You cannot hold on to the leaf very long; it flows by and disappears. Feelings also come and go. Do not cling to them.

The leaf that flows by is a good image, because it makes this visualization more concrete.

Feelings are "us," just as the drops of water are the river. But they are not all of us, just as those drops of water are not the whole river.

Each drop of water flows by and disappears, but the river is still there.

In the same way, each feeling comes, stays for a while, and goes, but we are still there observing.

Avoid slipping into the river of feelings. Remain dry.

If you fall in and find yourself in the river, do not struggle.

Just get back to your seat on the riverbank, and get back in touch with your breath.

As you return to observing the breath, the observer stance arises again.

The observer is not a critic. The observer is nonjudgmental. Better than that, the observer can be compassionate toward the one who has the feelings. She can be accepting toward her and her feelings. This makes the practice easier and more rewarding.

(This exercise is a meditation theme that depends on visualization. For this reason it is not included in the downloads.)

ONLY THE BREATH

Meditation practice starts with noticing that one is breathing, then continues with paying attention to one's breath. But it shifts into high gear only when "the one who is breathing" disappears and only the breathing remains. "The one who is breathing" is a story, and stories are in the mind. They also change according to who is telling the story and to whom. The story that is "you" as your mother tells it may be quite different from the way your mother-in-law tells it—and it may also be different from moment to moment, depending on how you feel about yourself. Sometimes even a witness in a court case changes her story. Your concentration on the breath will not be complete so long as your mind is full of the one who is breathing.

The Autopilot Mode

Recently, one participant remarked that she had just discovered a surprising ability to pay attention to the breath in the background while she continued to think! I had to tell her that this happens to all of us—the brain has the remarkable propensity to put repetitive activities on autopilot and switch its main focus to activities that exhibit more variety. Thus, we breathe on autopilot, walk on autopilot, drive on autopilot, and eat and drink on autopilot while the brain daydreams. And while doing that, we overeat and we drink too much. We also use more gas than we need to—I observe many drivers accelerating toward a curve or a stop sign. They are only aware that one pedal makes the car go, and the other makes it stop. They are not aware that those pedals also control how much smog there is in the air and have an effect on those environmentally damaging oil spills.

Unhappiness and the Autopilot Mode

When we give the brain free rein, it follows its own negativity bias and other entrenched habits. If the entrenched habits are stress, anxiety, or sadness, those are the places automatic thinking takes us. It's like a dog chasing its own tail—the more we think negative thoughts, the more negative thinking becomes a habit. The more it becomes a habit, the more often we think negatively. This is not exactly a recipe for happiness.

With mindfulness, we are not only present to others—we are also more present to ourselves. We become more intimate with ourselves. We know what we are thinking and feeling, and we can change the direction of our thinking. Mindful living is the opposite of living on autopilot.

PRACTICING WITH SONGS

Working with practice songs requires an open heart. If you are thinking of other things as you listen, or if you are busy evaluating or judging the songs, they will not penetrate your heart. These songs are written with the express purpose of bringing you positive energies and a fresh wind of change. Let them penetrate your being. Once you become familiar with a song, sing along, either mentally or vocally.

NOURISHING THE SPIRIT

Automatic thoughts do not always nourish the spirit. Sometimes they do the opposite. Start a meditation period with positive feelings such as love, gratitude, or appreciation for being alive. We can visualize all the good things in our lives and recognize and acknowledge them. Then, when we focus on our breathing, we may find that our positive feelings permeate each breath—we are basking in the sunshine of positive feelings. When undertaken in this spirit, meditation is a nourishing experience.

We can look at the practice songs in this book also as food for the spirit. Everything we do is some kind of nourishment—we are feeding either positive energies or negative energies in us. Becoming aware of this is a kind of awakening—every thought, every conversation, every piece of music is also nourishment. Think of practice songs as supplements and vitamins, because what we ordinarily get from our iPods or the radio may not always be nutritious enough.

THE LIVING BUDDHA

At the end of his life, Buddha exhorted his followers to internalize his teachings and follow the guidance of their own mindfulness energy. This internalized Buddha is the living Buddha. It wakes up with us when we wake up in the morning, has breakfast, goes to work, and helps kids with their homework in the evening.

It is a source of comfort, and it smiles with us as we observe our breathing, our feelings, and our thoughts. When we speak with mindfulness, we speak kindly—when we listen with mindfulness, we listen with an open and compassionate mind. If you make mindfulness energy your constant companion, you will live with less stress, less negativity, and more contentment. Although we all have mindfulness energy to some extent, we do not necessarily recognize it as such. The exercises in this book are designed to nourish that energy and make it a living force in your life.

3

POSITIVE RUMINATION, EARWORMS, AND MANTRAS

> *Awake. Be the witness of your thoughts.*
> *You are what observes, not what you observe.*
> —BUDDHA
>
> *Change your thoughts and you*
> *change your world.*
> —NORMAN VINCENT PEALE

There is a difference between how literary types use the word *rumination* and the way psychologists do. The dictionary defines *ruminate* as "think deeply about something," and ordinary usage often reflects that. There is even a literary periodical called *Ruminate*. There is nothing sinister about it—it is a quarterly magazine of short stories, poetry, creative nonfiction, and visual art.

The psychological definition, on the other hand, centers on focusing attention compulsively on the symptoms of one's distress and on its possible causes and consequences, instead of its solutions. How did this word get to have such a negative connotation in psychology? A cow does not ruminate selectively and only burp up thorns. A regular, run-of-the-mill mind also ruminates about all sorts of things. A cow needs to digest its food more than once, and we seem to have the same need for our thoughts. Perhaps psychologists have mostly seen the negative side of rumination as they have focused on treating mental illnesses, for it is rumination in the psychological sense that creates problems.

IF YOU WANT TO KNOW WHERE YOUR HEART IS, LOOK WHERE YOUR MIND GOES WHEN IT WANDERS

Following thoughts to see where they are leading can be a good way to get acquainted with the biases, preoccupations, and programming of our brains, but it is only a first step. When we are driving, we do not just go where the car takes us. We have a notion of where we *want* to go. If we are not familiar with the surroundings, we look at a map or check with Google Maps to see that we are indeed heading in the right direction. If necessary, we change course. U-turns are not that rare in unfamiliar territory.

We do not have to go where the brain wants to take us either. We can also change the direction of our lives. We can also make U-turns on the road of life. The brain may appear to have definite preferences and be set in its ways, but it is possible to talk back to it. Brain scientists assure us that the brain is plastic and can be molded to our purposes.

Do you have a map?

Do you know where you want to go?

As we mature, our road map also changes. Remember that there was a time when your mind went to Barbie dolls or toy cars when it wandered.

The brain may feel like a tyrant, but when you assert yourself, you may find that it can also be accommodating.

The saying "If you want to know where your heart is, look where your mind goes when it wanders" describes a bottom-up process, useful for becoming aware of what is actually happening now.

Let us revise it in a more proactive way: "Make sure that your heart is in the right place; then, when your mind wanders, it will go where you want it to go."

FOLLOW YOUR BLISS . . .

You may remember the popular Bill Moyers interviews with Joseph Campbell on PBS that popularized the saying "Follow your bliss." But how do we follow our bliss? By eating tons of chocolate ice cream? By sitting in front of the TV and watching sports all day? By zoning out with prescription painkillers?

Those activities may represent the "bliss" of the brain.

But following the road signs for brain heaven may actually lead to mind-hell.

When Joseph Campbell came out with that popular teaching, he was inspired by Indian spirituality, where bliss (or *Ananda*) is promoted as a desirable quality.

Ananda is a lovely word that has also become an attractive offbeat name in the West. However, in the Indian context, it is often an abbreviation for *Sat Chit Ananda*, which means something like "the bliss of pure consciousness"—in other words, the bliss of a mind that has been trained and purified by meditation, and not your regular chocolate-craving brain.

POSITIVE RUMINATION

Rumination control is one of the purposes of meditation. Here I am using *meditation* in the larger sense to stand for "spiritual practice." The Hare Krishnas who used to be a fixture on our downtown streets some time ago were practicing a form of positive rumination—mantra chanting is a form of positive rumination. There are also echoes of it in the *"Ave Maria"*'s chanted with prayer beads by Catholics. The German Kirtan singer Deva Premal has a large following, and American Kirtan singers such as Krishna Das and Snatam Kaur are also quite popular, and for a good reason. It is uplifting to participate in a session of Kirtan singing. The uplifting feeling comes from filling our hearts and minds with positive energy—Kirtans repeat the names of God, and God is conceived of as positive energy par excellence.

PRACTICE SONGS

I started writing practice songs out of a wish to bring the same kind of focused positive energy to mindfulness practice. I enjoyed the uplifting feeling of Kirtans but did not personally relate to Krishna, Rama, and other Indian gods and goddesses very strongly. I also wanted to use Western languages instead of an exotic and extinct foreign language such as Sanskrit. I wanted the words to carry their share of meaning without a dictionary. You will notice that some of the practice songs in this book are like mantras in that they have short texts that are repeated like a call-and-response song.

Using Songs for Personal Growth

Songs can help concentrate the mind and focus it in beneficial directions. Their usefulness is supported by a long tradition. If you want to use songs in your practice but feel somewhat limited by your own background, these examples may help. I know of one psychologist who occasionally "prescribes" specific practice songs from my previous collection, *Basket of Plums*, for her clients. Just asking a client "to meditate" may be too vague or too general a request. When suggesting a specific practice song for someone, it is best to introduce it in your own words first. Then, at the next session, you can ask for feedback, or ask specific questions referring to the content of the song. This book gives many examples of such explorations that go deeper into the meaning and purpose of a song.

Music is a powerful tool, both for personal growth and for therapy. Music therapy is a recognized academic discipline, but it has become a specialty mostly used in palliative care. Having these recorded songs ready to upload to an iPhone or portable digital music player can bring this tool into more general use and make it easier to use for everyone.

Harnessing the Power of Music

In an article in the *Oxford Journals*, Oliver Sacks describes watching the well-known composer Lukas Foss, who had Parkinson's disease, "rocket almost uncontrollably to his piano, but once he [was] there," playing "a Chopin nocturne with exquisite control and timing and grace," only to freeze or hurry back awkwardly as soon as the music ended. He adds that "the evocative power of music can also be of immense value in people with Alzheimer's disease or other dementias, who may have become unable to understand or respond to language, but can still be profoundly moved—and often regain their cognitive focus, at least for a while—when exposed to music, especially familiar music."

Music activates the emotions. Music and poetry can bring a roundness and completeness to an exclusively cerebral discourse. Emotions can also help us make decisions and influence the direction of our lives.

Practice songs are not meant to replace traditional instructions on getting started with meditation. They are meant to enrich your practice or help move it forward so it does not stagnate. If you are attending a meditation group or go to a retreat, there will be insights from talks or from sharing that will also open new vistas for you. Meditation practice needs to be periodically renewed and reinvigorated. If you feel "meditation inertia" at any time, find a way to inspire yourself. The practice songs in this book are offered in this spirit. Sing along with a song until it begins to speak to you. Hum it occasionally during the day. Each song emphasizes a different aspect of practice and will enrich your horizon as you make it your own.

Songs for Inspiration

Oprah recounts that for the occasion of his TV interview with her, Thich Nhat Hanh arrived at the studio accompanied by a group of monastics. This is how she describes the scene: "As we take a photograph together just before our chat, they usher in a peaceful mood by collectively singing a Buddhist song: 'We are all the leaves of one tree; we are all the waves of one sea; the time has come for all to live as one.'"

If you watch that interview, you may notice that the power of that collective practice comes through in Thich Nhat Hanh's presence. Indeed, music is used to illuminate every aspect of the practice at Plum Village, where Thich Nhat Hanh lives. The community sings before walking meditation, they sing before group discussions, and they sing before Thich Nhat Hanh's morning talks. Music is very much a part of the practice at Plum Village. With the songs in this book, you can make it a part of your practice as well.

PRACTICE SONG
"It's the Light That I Long For"

It's the light that I long for, not the clouds that I care for.
Here and now, or tomorrow, in the sky, in your eye,
See the light, not the clouds,
Here and now, or tomorrow, in the sky, in every eye.

This mantra is looking for the spark that redeems the whole. It is looking for that bright moment that "makes" the day, the spark in the eye and the little words of appreciation that "make" the relationship.

Is there no place for talking about your feelings if those feelings are not positive?

People often come to me in private sessions to talk about problem areas in their lives, the "clouds." And often I point them toward the light, either the light that is shining through the clouds or the light that is coming from other directions. It is there, but they do not look in the right place. And sometimes, in their preoccupation with problems, they neglect the importance of moving toward the light. Our heart's desire, what we want to do with our lives, our goals and values, can all be sources of light. As we move toward them, their light becomes stronger and clearer and shows us the way forward.

We can be mesmerized with darkness—the darkness that may be there in the past, or the darkness we anticipate in the future with anxious thoughts. But we may never be able to solve all the problems of the past! The way out of past problems is like a closed door—time has closed the door, and we bump into that closed door over and over again as we explore the dark areas of our past. Go to the past for a visit, go to enjoy the light if there is light there, but if all you encounter is darkness, don't stay there too long. Come back toward the light of the present.

The door of the future is not open yet. Is there light or darkness behind that closed door? That depends on you, to a large extent. You can bring light to the future, and then it will be bright. The future is waiting for the light. Don't waste too much time gazing into a crystal ball. If you look closely, you will notice that every crystal ball is also a mirror—there is a subtle reflection of your face on its surface.

Once, at the beginning of my journey with mindfulness, I asked a teacher how meditation practice had affected her friendships. Did she still have the same friends as before? Did she spend as much time with them?

"I no longer have friends who just complain" was her short answer.

Indeed, some people get together to complain—about work, about family, about politics, about anything and everything. Do they have "positivity blindness," or is it a habit? The Yiddish word for "complain" is *kvetch*. In *Born to Kvetch*, Michael Wex writes that for the practiced ones, "complaining is not only a pastime, not only a response to adverse or imperfect circumstances, but a way of life that has nothing to do with the fulfillment or frustration of desire. Kvetching can be applied indifferently to hunger or satiety, satisfaction or disappointment: it is a way of knowing, a means of apprehension that sees the world through cataract-colored glasses." That is the most eloquent description I have ever seen of how deeply ingrained an attitude can be.

Remember: When one side of the Earth is in darkness, the other side glows with light. "If the Sun and Moon should ever doubt, they'd immediately go out," said William Blake. An attitude such as positivity or negativity is not only a reflection of our life experience—it also shows how we experience life now and forecasts how we will experience it in the future.

4
WHOLEHEARTED LIVING

> *I promise myself that I will enjoy every minute of the day that is given to me to live.*
>
> —THICH NHAT HANH

Meditation reorients the mind. Ordinarily, the mind follows the messages that reflect the evolutionary, biological, or culture-induced interests of the brain. In meditation, we pay attention intentionally. Concentration is essential to meditation—think of walking a dog. The dog is constantly distracted by the cacophony of smells on the sidewalk—estimates vary, but a dog's nose is perhaps 100,000 times more sensitive than ours. As a consequence, the dog is suffering from information overload and is constantly darting this way or that as it "follows its nose." There are no estimates, but our brain is probably more powerful than a dog's brain by at least that amount. We also suffer from information overload.

Without intentional attention, we are at the mercy of the brain. Without concentration, our brain will also be darting around from thought to thought and miss the raw beauty of the nature that is all around us.

I often see dog walkers who are struggling with their dogs. They are pulling one way, and the dog is pulling the other, and a lot of energy is getting wasted in that struggle. They are like meditators who are straining on a leash. "Don't turn yourself into a battlefield," says Thich Nhat Hanh. A lot of energy is lost on a battlefield.

Then, occasionally, I come across a dog walker who seems to have a different species of dog—one that does not seem to follow its nose like the others and pull this way and that. It is appealing to watch, as it looks harmonious—the dog and its walker seem to be on the same wavelength. It looks effortless, but I have watched enough videos of Cesar Millan, the legendary "dog whisperer," to know that this is the result of training.

Mind training is the key to successful meditation.

Meditation teacher Sri Chinmoy said that people often want to know if they are meditating properly. His answer was, "It is very easy to know. If you are meditating properly, you will get spontaneous inner joy. Nobody has given you good news, nobody has brought you any gifts, nobody has appreciated or admired you, nobody has done anything for you, but you will have an inner feeling of delight. If this happens, then you know that you are meditating properly."

This is quite different from the struggle that some people experience.

But how does one succeed in concentrating without a struggle and meditating with joy? For, in the long run, the people who continue with their meditation practice are the ones who enjoy their practice.

At the start of her TV interview with Thich Nhat Hanh (which you can find on the Internet), Oprah remarked that she felt less stressed after being with him just for a few moments, and she asked him, "Are you always this content and peaceful?" Thich Nhat Hanh's answer: "This is my training, this is my practice, and we try to live every moment like that, relaxed, dwelling peacefully in the present moment, and respond to events with compassion."

She pursued with, "So, in a moment where you are perhaps going to miss a plane, or be late for an appointment, or something that is causing you to be stressful, you do *what*?"

Notice that we are only a few seconds into the interview, and Oprah has already shifted her focus to meditation in action—to how to bring the benefits of meditation to a life of action. She knows that her viewers are also interested in that.

Here is the answer: "I go back to my breathing and try to be in that moment deeply, because it is possible to handle every kind of event, and the essential thing is to keep the peace in yourself."

This is what Thich Nhat Hanh is perhaps best known for—for showing us how to live our daily lives with the same peace and concentration that we are able to muster on the meditation cushion. He is not only a meditation teacher but also a life coach, in the best sense of the term. In *The Long Road Turns to Joy*, he goes back to the words of the Buddha to describe meditation in daily life:

> *The Buddha was asked, "What do you and your disciples practice?" and he replied, "We sit, we walk, and we eat." The questioner continued, "But Sir, everyone sits, walks, and eats." The Buddha told him, "When we sit, we know we are sitting. When we walk, we know we are walking. When we eat, we know we are eating."*

In other words, the magic is not so much in *what* we are doing, but in *how* we are doing it.

Thich Nhat Hanh explains: "Most of the time we are lost in the past or carried away by the future."

Here, you can also add things from your own experience, such as it may be— thinking about work, worrying about health, fretting about not having enough money, making sexual fantasies, or regretting having paid too much for the car repairs. If you are a hang glider, feel free to add "daydreaming about my next flight."

When you do any of these things while you sit in meditation, you are not really meditating.

When you do them during the course of everyday activities, you are not living wholeheartedly. When you are eating, just eat. The food was planted and harvested with much care, transported with much effort, prepared and brought to your plate with much attention. At least do it the honor of enjoying it.

When you walk, enjoy the day—the people around you, your surroundings, and the sheer fact that unlike the twenty percent of us who are either disabled or too old, you can enjoy walking.

The basic instructions for wholehearted living are the same as for sitting meditation: Be here now, and be in your body and not your mind.

Here are some specific instructions for two other activities.

WALKING MEDITATION

Wouldn't it be interesting to visit another planet, say the planet Mars, take a walk, look around, and see what the scenery is like?

We are, in fact, on an amazing planet—the planet Earth. It is more interesting than the other planets because it has so many different life-forms. Its atmosphere turns the darkness of the airless sky of space blue. Birds streak through this sky, and sometimes also butterflies. Its soft winds caress our skin, and its colors enchant our eyes. Familiarity may not always breed contempt, as the proverb says, but it often breeds inattention. Let us look at this beautiful planet of ours as if for the first time, with new eyes, with surprise, and with wonder. We are travelers here, like all our sister beings. Let us get to know everyone else, make friends with them, and enjoy our time here. We are on a lovely planet, not only a "lonely planet."

We usually walk in order to get somewhere, but in walking meditation the destination is not the important thing—walking meditation is like those occasions when we go for a walk and walk just for the pleasure of walking. Can we infuse all the walking we do with the same relaxed spirit? Walking meditation is a journey without a destination. You can coordinate your steps and your breathing: Take two or three steps as you breathe in, and two or three steps as you breathe out. This will help you stay in touch with your breath as you pay attention to the physical sensations of walking. Don't look down—be open to and appreciate the people, the sky, the trees, or whatever else may be around.

EATING MEDITATION

We can turn every ordinary activity into a meditative act by transforming the activity from a goal-oriented one to a process-oriented one. We are not eating just to get it over with—we wish to savor every bite and enjoy the taste and texture of the food. Just as in other forms of meditation, we give what we are doing our full attention, not thinking of other things while we eat. This concentration will allow us to have a more conscious relationship with the food we are eating—where it comes from, its effects on our body and mind, and all the work and care it took to bring it to our plate.

PRACTICE SONG
"A Smile with Every Breath"

A smile with every breath, a flower with every step,
I've already arrived; I'm already at home.

Nature smiles in a flower. We smile with our face.

The flower is the eye-catching part of the plant, but the smile of nature is in every part of the plant—in its roots, its stem, and its cells, which are too small for us to see.

The smile on our face is the visible part of a smile. Connect the smile on your face with a smiling heart, a smiling mind, and a smiling body. A smile is body language. Our body speaks without words. It does not know any English. That is why everyone can understand body language. Even babies can understand it. Speak with your smile. Let your smile express your deepest feelings. Let the smile *be* your deepest feelings. Like the flower, *be* the smiling face of nature. And further, let the smile be your home. Let your breath be the expression of your smile. If you are sitting, come home to your smile with every breath. If you are walking, come home to your smile with every step. Do not let thoughts take you away from your smile. Let the smile be the expression of your life, like the flower is the expression of the life of the flowering plant.

When you are walking, take your smile with you. Thomas Edison said that the chief function of the body is to carry the brain around. Change that. Make "carrying the smile around" the chief function of the body.

In walking meditation, the destination of the walk is not an external place. It is an internal place, a state of mind. This state of mind is described as the feeling of being at home, as when we say, "I feel at home here." Can you take that satisfying feeling with you everywhere? Can you feel "at home" everywhere you go? With every step?

You can, if you stay in your senses.

You can, if you do not let your thoughts take you to the past or to the future.

In fact, this song is not only about walking. It can also be about driving, running, canoeing, swimming, or riding the bus or the train. When you have a physical destination in mind, you are not mentally *here*. You are already mentally at your destination. The mind is swift. It can go to places in a blink. As soon as you think of your destination, the mind is already there. But the body is slow. It is still here. If you allow the mind to separate from your body and jump ahead, you'll leave your body behind.

The first result of this is a feeling of impatience. When you look with your mental eye, you are there where you want to be. But when you look with your physical eye, you are still here. What a drag! The slow one is usually your own body, but not necessarily. It can be your toddler walking aimlessly with her tiny legs—it may look like she's going to take a few lifetimes to make it to the next corner.

It can be your car, idling in a traffic jam.

Splitting yourself in two can also make you speed and drive aggressively. Be *here* when you drive or walk—not *there*—and enjoy the ride.

When walking, say to yourself that you have arrived, not that you *will* arrive. And when you get in your car, don't say, "I will soon arrive"; say, "I have already arrived." If you do this systematically, you will be at home wherever you go. You will be in your home in your heart, in your body. You will be whole. And you will still go where you want to go. But you will go with a smile of contentment and a flower in your heart.

Want to take this further?

Be *here* as you eat your breakfast, not mentally already done and out the door.

5

MEET THE FLINTSTONES

We admit that we are like apes, but we seldom realize that we are apes.

—RICHARD DAWKINS

"Our modern skulls house a Stone Age mind," say Leda Cosmides and John Tooby, in *Evolutionary Psychology: A Primer*. "Generation after generation, for 10 million years, natural selection slowly sculpted the human brain, favoring circuitry that was good at solving the day-to-day problems of our hunter-gatherer ancestors— problems like finding mates, hunting animals, gathering plant foods, negotiating with friends, defending ourselves against aggression, raising children, choosing a good habitat, and so on. Those whose circuits were better designed for solving these problems left more children, and we are descended from them." No other work of fiction has captured the essence of the quoted paragraph better than

The Flintstones. The Flintstones was the most financially successful animated cartoon for thirty years, and the reruns were my daughter's favorite TV show when she was a preschooler. I would often drop everything and watch them with her. We were far from being alone in our enthusiasm for it—in 2013, *TV Guide* ranked it the second-greatest TV cartoon of all time. *The Flintstones* achieved its appeal by treating modern everyday concerns in a Stone Age setting. I never got tired of watching Fred and Wilma driving their Stone Age car—their attitudes seemed so perfectly natural and believable. I now see why. Like all good comedy, there was a generous measure of truth in it.

Watching episodes of *The Flintstones* had a strange effect on me: I began to see Wilma and Fred everywhere, not only behind the wheel but also walking on the street, shopping, and at Starbucks. There is a hilarious side to the juxtaposition of Stone Age accoutrements such as a huge slab of stone for a garage door with modern conveniences such as a telephone, or Stone Age clothes with a motorcycle cop who flags speeding cars. However, there is also a dark side that this comedy show understandably avoids. "The key to understanding how the modern mind works is to realize that its circuits were not designed to solve the day-to-day problems of a modern American—they were designed to solve the day-to-day problems of our hunter-gatherer ancestors," say Cosmides and Tooby. And I would add, "in a Stone Age manner." Indeed, the veil of civilization drops in war zones where Stone Age behavior is the norm. It also drops behind closed doors where conjugal violence happens, in prisons, in the streets and bars at night under the influence of alcohol, and in countries where barbarity against women is accepted.

But that is not all. Closer to home, the savage egotism of those Wall Street managers who caused the recent financial crisis and the club-wielding of some politicians who ruthlessly push for special interests and loopholes while ignoring the common good look suspiciously Stone Ageish to me. Look closer, and you will see it in more places—in the way cars are advertised, for example. And if you look closer still, you may finally recognize Stone Age attitudes in yourself— if not in your behavior, then in your emotions.

A poster at the Museum of Natural History in Miguasha National Park in Canada shows a fierce-looking dragonlike creature with a huge open mouth full of razor-sharp teeth. The caption underneath reads, *This cute creature is part of your genealogical tree*. Most visitors would look at this image with some amusement, without taking it personally. But Buddha showed us to take our fierce ancestors personally, because their shadows lurk inside, just below consciousness. Without mindfulness, their fierceness holds us under its sway.

BUDDHA AND EVOLUTIONARY PSYCHOLOGY

"After deeply entering meditation, he began to discern the presence of countless other beings in his own body in the present moment. Organic and inorganic beings, minerals, mosses, and grasses, insects, animals, and people were all within him. He saw that other beings were himself right in the present moment. He saw his own past lives, all his births and deaths. [. . .] He felt all the joys and sorrows of every living being."

This is how Thich Nhat Hanh describes Buddha's awakening in *Old Path, White Clouds*, his interpretive story of Buddha's life. According to Thich Nhat Hanh, in that moment, Buddha realized that all his previous lives were in him now—they were not merely past history. The Buddha saw that he was also all those beings in the present moment. This interpretation follows tradition, and it sees in Buddha the seeds of evolutionary psychology.

Understand the Past, but Do Not Get Stuck in It

With mindfulness, the past colors the present; it colors our understanding of the present, but it does not dictate our actions. On the contrary, knowing the past can be a warning that without mindfulness, the same urges of our evolutionary ancestors can overwhelm us at any moment. Buddha did not go on to follow the demons from the past in his actions, as many historical tyrants and emperors have done.

Buddha's approach can be an inspiration for psychodynamic psychotherapies as well. Understanding the personal past, the events and the traumas of child-

JOSEPH EMET • 63

hood, brings insight, but it also underlines the importance of mindfulness practice because, in the end, it is mindfulness practice that liberates a person from the grip of the past. The past influences the present through habit. We automatically think or react in a certain way now because of our past conditioning. Without mindfulness, we can just continue being the same way, thinking the same way, feeling the same way, and blaming it all on past events. Mindfulness makes it possible to make fresh tracks. At first, we gingerly walk on those fresh tracks. With time, the tracks deepen, new habits form, and change becomes a reality.

The View from the Top of the Pyramid

For most of us, evolution means being at the top of the intelligence pyramid. But I think a case could be made for seeing ourselves at the top of the cruelty pyramid as well. Despite their fierce looks, none of our animal ancestors had the unbelievable cruelty of the Khmer Rouge or the Nazis. And this is just in recent memory. Our animal ancestors killed one another mostly for food. We kill for more abstract, ideological reasons. And mindfulness has become even more essential at this juncture—some time ago, it was hard work to kill somebody. You had to approach the person and run a sword through him. With the invention of the gun, it became easier to kill—all you had to do was to pull a trigger from a distance. Now, that trigger controls a nuclear weapon. During those world wars, the monkeys in our zoos must have been scratching their heads even more than usual and wondering why they were imprisoned in cages while the most violent species in the history of the Earth was roaming free. We need to own and accept our fierceness. We need to become aware of it in order to exert some control over it; otherwise it will control us from the dark corners of our unconscious. That fierce, dragonlike creature at the nature museum in Miguasha National Park did not only live in the remote past; it lives in us now. It shows its sharp teeth not only in wartime but in also in our "peacetime" murders, rapes, and bullying.

We are at the top of the evolutionary pyramid not only in terms of intelligence but also in terms of many other qualities—including stress and anxiety. Buddha recognized that he had an evolutionary brain, with all the urges, emotions, and reactions that come with it. Buddha recognized but did not identify with the voice of his evolutionary brain. He identified with his *mind*, and defined the energy we know as mindfulness.

When I was in high school, evolution was presented to us as if we humans grew out of beings such as rats and monkeys, but we had now magically left all that behind. We were now human, a different sort of being. We had *evolved*. But denying the dark side of the evolutionary reality of the human brain deprives us of the first essential step of mindfulness—that of recognition. If we do not recognize and acknowledge the urges and biases that come with having an evolutionary brain, we cannot go beyond them—we become prisoners of them.

"The Devil Made Me Do It"

Our nonangelic side is so evident that some version of the Devil had to be invented by religions in order to explain it. One unfortunate result of this was that the mind soon became a battleground between the forces of good and evil, and fighting with the Devil only made it a stronger presence for us. In contrast to this, the journey of mindfulness starts with acceptance. We cannot change the Devil, we can only change ourselves.

Another downside of substituting the Devil for the evolutionary brain is that while the evolutionary brain speaks with the experience of having evolved on this planet, the Devil is only one letter away from evil, and good and evil have often been arbitrary and self-serving concepts.

GUIDED MEDITATION
The Mirror Mind

When a mountain lake is agitated by winds, the moon that is reflected in it appears in a dozen broken pieces. In it, clouds look distorted, and trees dance.

Taking three deep and slow breaths, I calm my mind and body.

I visualize a calm lake reflecting everything like a mirror.

The moon in the lake is in one piece, and the clouds look the same as they do in the sky.

When my mind is calm, it is like that lake, reflecting things as they are.

As I calm my mind, the outside world also feels calmer; things appear simpler and easier to deal with.

Calm mind, calm world: just trees, just clouds, and just the moon.

My mind reflects things as they are.

The steady rhythm of my breath calms me, like the hand that gently rocks the cradle calms a fussing baby.

I let that calmness pervade my whole body and mind.

I sit basking in pleasant feelings that come from a relaxed body and mind.

Mental states are like cloud formations in the sky.

They depend on the winds of emotion and thought, and change from moment to moment.

States of mind such as certainty, uncertainty, or irritation come
and go.
I watch them arise and disappear.

Without breath-awareness, a mental state can take up all the
space.
Focusing on my breath creates space in my mind.

I make room for my feelings as I observe and accept them.
As I sit, there is just sitting.
As I breathe, just breathing.

On a clear summer day, everything is bathed in light.
The light of my awareness shines like the sun.

6

RIDING DRAGONS AND EMBRACING TIGERS

> *Everybody says that I'm a man,*
> *but I'm not so sure.*
> *Sometimes I think I'm also a mother.*
>
> **—THICH NHAT HANH**

Are men's brains and women's brains telling their owners different things?

As Dr. Louann Brizendine and others who have studied female and male brains point out, our brains are indeed different. It would be surprising if our different brains gave us identical messages.

I have a picture of a female figure riding a dragon from a Korean temple—as she stands serenely on the dragon, she holds a vial of the "water of compassion" in one hand and sprinkles it on the Earth with the other. Perhaps, in portraying her on a dragon, the ancients thought that a woman's body is a little harder to "ride" than a man's body. This is no doubt still true of women who experience

PMS or those who have a hard time with pregnancy or menopause. Yet, this rider, Quan Yin, Tara, Chenrezig, or Avalokiteshvara, as her many variations are called in different Buddhist lands, is distributing compassion while balancing on the dragon. Her drops of compassion fall on babies, children, the elderly, the sick, and whoever happens to come by. What also impresses me is that she is not at all unbalanced or preoccupied by the dragon she is standing on. She seems to have a good relationship with it.

What dragon are you riding?

Laurie came to meditation because she was becoming aware that her controlling attitude was having a negative influence on her family. The example she gave me was that she was trying to dictate every little thing to her husband, like how to do the laundry or how to wash the dishes. If you also have the "control gene," you will immediately understand how she feels. If you do not, you may be puzzled that "such a small thing" loomed large in her life. It was not a small thing for her or her family.

It is not an outstanding feat to find your balance while standing on the sidewalk. You do not even need practice in order to do it. The challenge is to find your balance while standing on a dragon. Laurie came to see that the name of her dragon was *Control*. That is the first step of recognition, or awareness. Her next step would be to find equanimity on the dragon. Again, it is one thing to find equanimity when there are no dragons around, and another to find it while riding one. I encouraged her to make friends with her dragon and not to treat it unkindly. Many successful people have issues with control, for it is through self-control that they have achieved success in life. It is through self-control that Laurie has a slim figure, and it is through self-control that her spending and finances are in good order. Successful people have experienced the positive side of control at school and at work—now they have to see that letting go can also be a positive quality. They also need to see that there is a difference between self-control and control of others.

Being self-critical is another character trait that is essential for success in many professions and trades. Self-criticism may have had a positive effect on the success of a good actress, and she may think that being critical of others will be helpful to them in the same way that it has helped her. It is easy to be attached to a trait that has brought you success, money, and recognition, and it is natural to value it highly. Any such highly valued trait can become second nature. But being critical of your partner does not earn you brownie points in a relationship.

CLOSING THE GENDER GAP

Evolution may not have destined us for relationship heaven.

It is possible that men evolved to get along well with other men rather than with women. Men who could bond with other men and join hunting, raiding, and attacking parties had an evolutionary advantage. Many servicemen cherish the close bond of camaraderie that develops in war zones—they prize that camaraderie over anything they can find in peacetime society. Many join the army voluntarily and return for extra tours of duty even after being wounded. Street gangs, the mafia, and terrorist organizations also bear witness to this male tendency to bond with other males to pursue a common purpose.

Our evolutionary past may not have primed us for world peace either. The struggle for alpha-male status is a way of life among many animals. We descended from those who won that struggle. Our ancestors fought for reproductive supremacy, not for world peace or a sustainable lifestyle.

Loving relationships and a peaceful world are dreams of mindfulness, not of "brainfulness." Happy, long-lasting relationships are the exception rather than the rule among couples—you do not need them in order to fulfill nature's goal of reproduction. All you need is sexual attraction, and nature provided us with plenty of that. Opposites attract, but they also destroy each other. Attraction is enough to make babies, but to make loving relationships, women and men also need to understand, cherish, and move toward each other.

Men ride a male dragon. Evolution molded us to fight, to compete, and to dominate. With the spark that we received from our past, we explored continents and built railroads, ships, airplanes, and airports. We mined metals and coal to make life more comfortable. We discovered medicines to increase our life spans and cure many illnesses. Now we need to learn the art of observing our evolutionary urges without feeling compelled to act them out. We need to recognize and accept them and go beyond them toward peaceful coexistence and flourishing relationships. Women have embraced certain male values such as work-place competition and independence and moved closer to men—to realize the extent of this change, watch some movies from the fifties or read a Victorian novel. Women have also learned to run marathons and climb Mt. Everest. Men need to move closer to women also and embrace some of their values, such as compassionate parenting, noncompetitive relationships, and a taste for emphatic encounters. Those values are important in good relationships and for world peace.

This is an important part of the journey toward mindfulness described through-out this book. Ernest Hemingway's *Men without Women* is a set of stories about aggressive, violent, and sometimes criminal men. These stories illustrate what happens when men live by their evolution-driven brains and values. Those values are still alive in us—we are still coasting along on the thrust we received from millions of years of evolution. Mindfulness makes it possible to recognize them if and when they surface, and know that they belong to the dragon. Then they lose their compelling quality on the person who is riding the dragon. It also helps to steer the dragon toward calmer pastures and not to feed it with the media violence that is constantly spilling out from our computers and TV sets. Watching violent "sports" and action movies and playing certain kinds of computer games water the seeds of violence and allow them to come closer to the surface.

Books about gender differences mostly describe the dragons we ride. They do not describe the riders who have balanced on their dragons and followed their values. Those who did have transcended their evolutionary gender roles as well as roles assigned to them by culture. "Work is love in action," said Gandhi. "Work, so that you can buy more things," says our culture. "Work, so you will be more successful," says another voice inside me. "Time is money" is the message of our work environment. "Time is not money, time is love," says Thich Nhat Hanh. I sit quietly so that I can hear all these voices clearly. We need to develop a peaceful heart in order for love to show in our actions.

PRACTICE THEME
Developing a Peaceful Heart

There are many voices everywhere, even on the radio. One moment, my radio says, "Help with this fund-raising effort for women in distress," and the next moment it says, "Go to this big party."

In the morning, the teenage boy hears, "Sleep some more" from his brain.

He also hears, "Go to class,"

and "Go with the gang."

What voices did *you* hear this morning? What voices do you hear now? Which is louder? Which is "you"?

Voices come from different parts of the body and brain, from media culture, and from our family culture. We are always at the crossroads, and there is stress, even when there is no stress.

The brain makes up all the words. Let go of all the words coming from the brain.

Bring your attention lower, to the abdomen that breathes wordlessly.

Peace Is Every Breath, said Thich Nhat Hanh.

That is a meditation theme, a mantra.

Practice with that mantra until you experience freedom.

Then sit wordlessly, and listen wordlessly.

Calm the body and the mind, and find serenity.

When you get up, do what needs to be done.

Do it with compassion, and with mindfulness.

OF BEING AND DOING

The world of music offers a good model for envisaging our differences as well as our similarities as women and men. In a choir, women and men are different and complementary, but in an orchestra they are similar and independent. In a choir, men cannot do what women can do, and vice versa, but in an orchestra, each gender can do whatever the other can. An all-women choir and an all-men choir have distinctly different sounds, but you cannot tell an all-men orchestra from an all-women orchestra by sound alone. It all boils down to the fact that the voice is part of the being of a person, whereas playing an instrument is part of their doing.

Meditation has to do with being. Do not turn it into some kind of doing.

My partner, Suzanne, is fond of watching couples figure skating competitions. I used to tease her about being a romantic at heart, but as I watched some of her favorite programs with her, I began to see that there is more going on there than presumed romance between the skating couple.

Firstly, there is seamless cooperation, and the joy of working wholeheartedly toward a common goal. *Her* competence improves *his* chances of winning, as *his* competence improves *hers*. The sense of "me" and "you" merge into a tangible sense of "we."

Secondly, they do everything with a smile. There is effort, there is planning, and there must be some concern about making a misstep—but these are all submerged under the positive feelings implied by the smile. If you think this is a superficial matter, try it. Try doing your exercise routine at the gym with a smile. Lift weights, do pushups, run, and spin with a smile. Then drive home with a smile, and when you get home, do the dishes with a smile. You will notice the profound difference this "superficial" detail makes in how you feel, and on your stress level.

No less important is how gender differences play out. The man and the woman are equally skillful yet play different roles appropriate for their physiques. The man supports the woman. He provides a steady and dependable base for her to soar, defy gravity, and add magic to their common presentation. Too often in marriages of the past, there has been a woman behind every successful man. Perhaps one of the things Suzanne finds charming in figure skating is the consistent reversal of this role. In the world of figure skating, it is the man who *always* supports the woman. In a good relationship and in good parenting, providing support is a role that shifts from partner to partner as the context demands. Unfortunately, the rules of parenting and relationships are not as clear as those of couples skating. However, mindfulness, not only of one's own needs but also of the needs of one's partner as well as of the situation, can take the place of the missing rulebook.

Mindfulness is a human quality like courage or kindness that we all have to some degree. However, in many of us, it is buried under other qualities that our culture promotes more actively, such as greed or ambition. But outstanding individuals like Buddha, and in our time Thich Nhat Hanh, have focused on that precious quality and displayed it prominently for all to see. They have also taught ways to cultivate it so that we may all enjoy its benefits.

Here is a related metaphor from the Taoist tradition:

EMBRACE TIGER, RETURN TO MOUNTAIN

I will gather and scoop in all my assets from outside and from within.
I embrace my tiger and return to my mountaintop. I survey my
panoramic vision and shout with my heart full of joy.
I kick up my heels and soar. I feel just fine.

This quotation is from *Embrace Tiger, Return to Mountain*, Al Huang's book on T'ai Chi practice. The title refers to a short sequence in the T'ai Chi form starting with the arms folded over the chest as if embracing something, and ending with a turn and an opening of the arms in a slant mimicking a mountain. Al Huang's fanciful interpretation hits the mark, for the only tiger one could really embrace without getting bloodied is the tiger inside, and that is the connection to the preceding dragon metaphor. As the practitioner returns to "mountain," he finds other qualities such as stability and peace there.

Al Huang continues with, "I will gather and scoop all my assets from outside and from within"; then the tiger is no longer alone to dominate. "I survey my panoramic vision"; my vision is no longer restricted by my aggressiveness or other qualities of the tiger. I can see 360 degrees, all around.

In my own twenty-five years of T'ai Chi practice, balancing my Yang and Yin, my aggressiveness and softness, was a new challenge during every practice period. I embraced my tiger and returned to mountain over and over again.

When I was young, I saw my parents struggle with the dragons and tigers I describe in this chapter. My mother had dysmenorrhea, and, at times, her painful periods absorbed much of her energy. My father was preoccupied with his political ambitions and battles and with his career successes and reversals. His double occupation as politician and MD absorbed his attention all the time. As I write these lines, I am surprised by how closely their lives reflected the topic of this chapter.

GENDERED MINDFULNESS

We are not abstract stick figures—we are gendered women and men. We were not children—we were girls and boys. When we were young, our relationships were with mothers and fathers, not with "parents." Our sexuality and the way it colors our relationships is at the center of our happiness as well as our unhappiness, our resilience as well as our fragility, our childhood and adolescence as well as our adult lives. Mindfulness practice guides us gently toward articulating our values and living by them. Following in the footsteps of the Buddha means balancing gracefully on the back of a dragon while leading a life of compassion and understanding.

GUIDED MEDITATION
Directing My Attention

I sit with good posture, and take a few deep breaths,
staying with each breath through the whole cycle of in breath
and out breath.

I become aware of the quality of my breath.
Is there calmness in the way I breathe?

I identify the feelings that I have as I breathe in and out.
I notice how my feelings come alive with each breath.
I breathe in and breathe out feelings.

Now, I'm consciously breathing with an awareness of calm and
peace.

I breathe in peace and breathe out peace.

There is nothing to do and no obligations now.

I allow myself to smile and to rest.

I bring my attention from my eyes and my head
where images and thoughts occur, down toward my abdomen
where breathing happens.

I do not try to stop the flow of images and thoughts up in my
head.

My attention now is on my expanding and contracting abdomen.

Breathing in, and breathing out,
I follow the calm, rhythmic motion of my abdomen.

Now, I *am* my breathing abdomen;
I'm not the amusement park in my head.

I take slower and deeper breaths,
      and notice all the different sensations of breathing.

As long as I'm with these sensations and my breathing,
I'm in my body. I'm at home in my body.

My breathing abdomen is my center.
I savor the delicious feeling of being alive.

My abdomen expands and contracts, expands and contracts,
      sending waves of awareness through my whole body.

I'm aware of my face muscles that react to every thought.
It's as if I think with my face muscles as much as with my brain.

I listen to the sensations from my legs.
I do not interpret them as messages of discomfort.

My sitting posture is stable and firm, like a small mountain.
I am not disturbed by thoughts that come and go.

7

ANTHROPOLOGY

> *Anthropology demands the open-mindedness with which one must look and listen, record in astonishment, and wonder that which one would not have been able to guess.*
>
> —MARGARET MEAD

While traditional religions study God, Buddhism studies human nature. That makes it closer to anthropology than to a religion.

But unlike the science of anthropology, the aim of Buddhism goes beyond understanding and describing human nature; its aim is also to provide tools for reducing suffering and stress and to describe pathways to happiness and contentment.

Mindfulness meditation is the most important of these tools.

Meditation is both a tool for self-discovery and an instrument for change.

Self-discovery starts as we first notice what a busy place the mind is. A little later, we begin to become more intimate with the workings of the mind as we notice where it goes when it wanders. Notice that this is already a metaprocess—we are already observing the mind objectively. Mindfulness is already there.

At about this time, it becomes also an instrument for change, because the observer's stance makes it possible to influence the brain instead of just being influenced by it.

An anthropologist is also a participant as well as an observer—she has trained herself to look at humans objectively, yet she is also a human. Being a participant gives the anthropologist firsthand knowledge of the experience of being a human—a Martian observer would lack that subjective sense of participation, and without that, it might find human behavior incomprehensible. On the other hand, a human who lacks the observant attitude of an anthropologist or a meditator can get so wrapped up in her own impulses and attitudes that she acts them out instead of contemplating them objectively.

Our first purpose in meditating is to see ourselves as we really are. One important difference between a meditator and an anthropologist is that the meditator first looks inside—she looks at *this* human—whereas an anthropologist mainly looks outside—at other humans.

SATIPATTHANA SUTTA

One of the key Buddhist texts on mindfulness is the *Satipatthana Sutta* (*Sutta* refers to a discourse of the Buddha). It starts with mindfulness of the breath and mindfulness of the body—important preludes, as most of us are in our minds much of the time. Attention to the body includes attention to posture, to how we hold the body and how we walk. Every movement of the body, such as bending down, is included as an object of awareness. Mindfulness lessons are not only abstract principles—I have benefited much from careful attention to my posture. I have an "unstable spine" that is just itching for an excuse to go out of whack. I have learned to be conscious of my center, my balance, and my posture as I bend down, carry things, or reach for something. This has allowed me to refrain from needlessly stressing my spine and spared me much pain.

The *Sutta* urges us to be aware of the body in the body. However, we are usually aware of the body as it is reflected in the mirror of the mind—through the judgments and interpretations of the mind. We even perceive pain through the mind: We feel words such as *terrible*, *awful*, and *unbearable* instead of the direct wordless sensations of pain. This is not feeling the body in the body—it is feeling the body as it is reflected in the mind. This distinction has important practical uses in pain management.

The next section deals with awareness of how the brain reacts to pleasant sensations—by wanting them to continue or to be repeated as often as possible.

This is a feedback loop—from the sense organs to the brain, and back to the sense organs over and over again. Pleasant sensations: Act to get more of the same. More pleasant sensations: Act to get more still. That is how we become obese, diabetic, or alcoholic. Only mindfulness can interrupt the cycle by enlarging the context to include values, goals, and a consideration of the effect of this loop on the body.

The brain reacts to unpleasant sensations by wanting them to stop, or by not wanting them to be repeated. What about "No pain, no gain"? Without the involvement of some measure of mindfulness, the brain would automatically veto that and say, "Give me more pleasant sensations, not this yucky stuff."

The brain has no automatic reaction toward sensations that are neither pleasant nor painful; if housecleaning or dishwashing does not result in awesome sensations, do not expect the brain to motivate you. You'd have to find your motivation elsewhere.

THE FIVE HINDRANCES AS BRAIN MESSAGES

The Buddha listed five hindrances to concentration and meditation.

1. SENSUAL THOUGHTS
   Coming to our senses is part of mindfulness practice. Daydreaming about sensual experiences is not.

There is a world of difference between the two.

Coming to our senses is part of being in the moment. When we are open to the senses, we are in the moment, for our senses give us information about the present moment.

Being caught in sensual thoughts, on the other hand, takes us away from the moment. It takes us back to, or forward to, a remembered or imagined sensual experience. This is true whether the sensual experience in question is the memory or anticipation of a sexual encounter or that of the taste of chocolate ice cream.

Come back to your breathing and to your senses in the present moment.

2. ILL WILL

When we build a campfire, we are conscious that we are continually feeding it branches and logs. With a propane stove, the process is automatic; we do not have to do anything—the fire seems to just continue burning by itself, but that's only because we may not be keeping in mind that the stove has a mechanism that creates a continuous supply of propane to the nozzle.

The fires of ill will also need thoughts of ill will to keep them burning, but we may not realize that we are the one who keeps feeding the flames. Thoughts and feelings of ill will just seem to perpetuate themselves. The first step is recognition of how we are feeding the fire. When we change the direction of our thoughts, the feelings will also change.

How do we change direction? We can see the other person also as a victim—a victim of her upbringing, beliefs, or culture. We can look for a good side—few people are wholly bad. Or we can simply realize that our hostile feelings are disturbing us more than they are hurting the other person—she may even be unaware that we have such feelings.

One way or another, try to reconnect with your inner smile and your natural friendliness. Other people do not control you without your consent.

3.   DROWSINESS

I have noticed that in every meditation group there is usually somebody who feels drowsy and somebody else who feels restless. They are in the same room, apparently doing the same thing, but no doubt the attitude is different.

Some beginners try to "just sit and relax" in meditation. There is no focus, no concentration. Yet there is more to meditation than just relaxation. Meditation starts with observing our breath and our physical sensations. One must be awake and paying attention in order to do that. If you feel yourself slipping into torpor, pay attention to your posture. The head feels heavier by about ten pounds for each inch that it is out of alignment with the spine. The resulting tension spreads to the shoulders. Abandoning your attention to posture ends up creating tension rather than relaxation.

4. RESTLESSNESS

Restlessness is sometimes felt as a physical urge to move and sometimes as the effect of accumulated issues of worry and dissatisfaction. The two are often related. Looking into the sources of our restlessness is rewarding.

The Buddha is often portrayed sitting on lotus flowers. This beautiful image says something about his state of mind. Thich Nhat Hanh asks us to notice if our meditation period feels like we are sitting on hot coals. If there is such a feeling of discomfort, where does it come from?

Only you can answer that question. Finding and owning the reasons of your restlessness will liberate you from them.

5. DOUBT

Doubt is the opposite of conviction. In practical terms it means a lukewarm interest. In order to see doubt as a kind of brain spam, one needs to take a certain distance from the doubt, because to reap the far-reaching benefits of mindfulness meditation, some amount of commitment to practice is needed. Doubt makes commitment difficult.

Many sections of this book are written with the express purpose of overcoming your doubts about the purpose and efficacy of mindfulness meditation. Doubt saps your energy and prevents you from applying yourself to meditation practice wholeheartedly.

Your brain is producing these five hindrances. Do not let them stop you from pursuing your meditation practice. What is your "favorite hindrance"? As you make friends with it and get to recognize it, it will lose much of its power to get in your way. The hindrances are opportunities for looking deeply. Instead of stewing in ill will, look deeply to explore its roots. Instead of letting doubt turn you away, use it analytically to ask the burning questions that animate your inquisitive spirit. Then the five hindrances will help move your practice forward instead of obstructing it.

LANGUAGE CAN MISLEAD

Just as language and how we use language comes under the scrutiny of anthropologists, it also comes under the gaze of the Buddha. "We are scared because of our notions of birth and death, increasing and decreasing, being and non-being.

Nirvana means extinction of all notions and ideas. If we can become free from these notions we can touch the peace of our true nature," writes Thich Nhat Hanh in his book *No Fear, No Death*. "The Buddha said, 'My teachings are a finger pointing to the moon. Do not get caught in thinking that the finger is the moon. It is because of the finger that you can see the moon.'"

Language can also amplify negative emotions by making an imaginary or remembered threat become omnipresent. An animal is not despondent about death. It does not know what death is, and it does not have a word for it. Our linguistic ability makes us think of death and become afraid of it over and over again every time that word comes to mind.

Did a person make you suffer deeply? You may suffer again and again every time you hear his name. The fact that there are taboo words in some cultures also attests to the power of words. But we do not have to go far to find taboo words; they exist in our culture also. We have words that are taboo on television or on political speeches.

In contrast, consider the following poem:

Life is
what is left
when you take away the words

When you walk
without words

like a child walks to her mother
when you watch the mystery
without making up a story. (J. E.)

PRACTICE SONG
"You're a Leaf on the Tree of Life"

You're a leaf on the tree of life,
For a season, its joy and pride,
In the fall, you lose your hold,
Give the tree back its gold.
Enjoy your day in the summer sun,
In the wind, wave hello,
In the fall, let go,
Give the tree back what you owe.

The Tree of Life is an image that has inspired many artists and craftsmen. I have seen lovely versions of it in Thailand and in Latin America with birds, butterflies, and squirrels on its branches and gazed at them with pleasure and appreciation.

But here, it is not only a metaphor; it is also is a practice theme. That distinction is important—it is the difference between esthetic appreciation and personal meaning. See yourself as a leaf on the tree of life; *be* that leaf that is here for only a season. Feel both the freshness and the greenness of the leaf and its ephemeral nature as your own. Notice that doing this gives a new urgency to appreciating the moment. And then practice with that insight.

Our life is our most precious and intimate possession. We see it as belonging to us. Yet this song says that our life is not entirely in us, but it is also part of a larger whole, in both time and space. When we truly see that, then some of the sense of preciousness that we ascribe to our own self, to our own life, will leak out toward that larger whole. We'll share that sense of preciousness with other beings and other selves. We will value our environment in a more personal way.

When we are at the prime of life, we rule the Earth. That is our day in the sun. We make babies and take care of them. We pay the taxes that take care of the elderly and send children to school. We pick up the garbage and govern countries. However, let us remember that we are not alone; we derive much of our power from other beings. Let us acknowledge that by waving.

Then, at some point, we begin to lose our hold just as the leaves on a real tree do.

Now, just like the once-lush green leaves, we will turn into compost. Like it or not, that is how a new generation will view us as they take over the Tree of Life. Compost nourishes the tree. The wisdom of past generations no longer governs us, but it still nourishes us. It has now been transformed to be relevant to present circumstances. Isaac Newton and his old physics have turned into compost. Even Einstein is slowly turning into compost as new theories address old problems more elegantly.

The second verse adds a nuance at the end: Do not cling to life, or you will be unhappy as it inevitably slips between your fingers. Let go mentally as well. On a real tree this letting go happens spontaneously, so this warning is addressed more specifically to metaphoric leaves. Many people approach the end of their lives with feelings of resentment. They may feel that they haven't taken enough. They are still hungry for more. Although this is easy to understand, it also brings some bitterness.

In contrast, being grateful for a good life well lived, for our day in the summer sun, wraps us up in pleasant feelings of contentment and gratitude.

It is better to go that way.

8

A RAINBOW OF FEELINGS

The earth laughs in flowers.

—RALPH WALDO EMERSON

The constant gray of depression, the continually flashing red lights of anxiety, and the ceaseless yellowish smog of some popular music contrast sharply with the full range of hues of a rainbow, the exuberance of colors in a flowering meadow, or the richness of tones in a blooming garden. In a free heart, the full range of feelings manifests, not only those that escape the censoring of society, culture, business, or the self. And they come and go like the changing vistas of the sky. Our changing feelings are illuminated by the gladness of being alive. A person who lives skillfully chooses her colors from this wide palette for the work of art that is her life.

The aggressive tendencies of the human brain won out in twenty million U.S. households that experienced domestic violence last year—the brain can be a dangerous organ. It can get addicted easily—more than twenty-three million Americans are addicted to drugs or alcohol. It can have poor taste and prefer unhealthy foods that make us sick. To make our life into a work of art, it is not enough to resist the pressures coming from big pharma and agribusiness—at times we must also resist the pressures coming from our own brain. We sometimes must go against its preferences and its particular interests—we must consider the well-being of our whole body, our family, our community, and our environment. In a word, we must be mindful that brains can have a narrow focus—they have evolved that way through the pressures of countless centuries of life in the wild. They still have some primitive features.

LOVE AND KINDNESS

"Everybody's got a story that would break your heart," says a song by Amanda Marshall. The title echoes Buddha's first noble truth, that suffering is omnipresent. How do we respond to this ubiquitous suffering and to the heartbreaking stories that are all around us? Do we listen with a heart like stone, or with a heart full of compassion?

Compassion, loving-kindness, or simply kindness as the Dalai Lama seems to prefer, is a big part of Buddhist practice, and it follows directly from that first noble truth about the universal nature of suffering. We do not have to wait to be told the heartbreaking story—we can just assume that it is there, and more often than not, we will be right.

Kindness is not only the heart's reaction to suffering—it is also an antidote to anger. In a recent group, several mothers shared that they often got irritated with their children, and their anger showed. They were concerned about how this would affect a young child, and they wanted to know if there was an easy way of being angry less often. I introduced them to Loving-Kindness Meditation. If you fill your heart with love and consciously hold loving-kindness in your heart, there is less room for anger to gain a foothold. The following song is one way of invoking the energy of love.

PRACTICE SONG
"Heal Yourself with the Mind of Love"

Heal yourself with the mind of love;
if you have enough love you are free.
—INSPIRED BY A TALK BY THICH NHAT HANH

Love is a healing energy, healing each one, healing couples, families, and communities. You might have encountered Zen teachings where enlightenment is presented as the goal of practice. You might think that enlightenment is mental and love is emotional, that they are different.

You may be surprised to know that Thich Nhat Hanh, in his book *Cultivating the Mind of Love*, describes the mind of enlightenment *as* the mind of love and affirms, "Awakening to our mind of love is the moment the practice begins."

Perhaps you were awakened to love when you encountered the love of your life. For each of us, there is someone out there with the key to unlock the door of our heart. They casually open the door, walk in, and make themselves at home. Then, from that day on, you are a lover. Your heart has become a few sizes bigger. It has expanded permanently. Perhaps it was a man or a woman who first unlocked your heart. Perhaps it happened when your baby was born and you held her in your arms. Cherish that sweet awakening. Do not stop there. Let your love expand and embrace all people, all flowers and birds, and the whole green Earth. Come back to love as to an oasis when you feel parched and dry. Make love a practice—a healing practice.

"Heal yourself with the mind of love," because we are all sick in varying degrees with the mind of exclusion or indifference, the mind of stress, and the mind of resentment or anger. Love brings with it a sense of inclusion, a longing for union, and a feeling of wholeness—of healing.

RUMINATION

The mind of love also short-circuits rumination. With a loving attitude, it is easier to accept the shortcomings of others or our own imperfections. Without it, we can be mired in repeating thoughts such as, "How could he do this to me?" or, "Why did I ever say that?" According to a recent study published in the journal *PLOS ONE*, "Rumination is the biggest predictor of depression and anxiety and determines the level of stress people experience." The mind of love makes forgiveness easier, and it turns our focus toward the beauty that is also there in the world, if we open our eyes a little wider (for a different look at rumination and its positive aspects, see chapter 3).

"If you have enough love you are free."

A person who is fixated on her anger is not free!

Angry thoughts roam wild and hold sway in an angry mind.

Anger often involves a wish to harm the object of our anger.

The mind of love creates a sort of immunity against grudges, resentments, and bitterness so that such thoughts do not gain a foothold as easily.

ANGER

We usually choose where we want to go. Imagine all of a sudden finding yourself in Afghanistan without any recollection of having made a decision or preparations to go there. One moment you are in the familiar surroundings and comforting emotions of your home, in, say, New York, and the next moment you find yourself in a war zone facing hostile emotions, and you do not know how you arrived there.

Anger can be like that. We become angry without choosing to, and often without a clear idea of how we got there. And we end up with bad feelings, and often also with dented personal relations. You may feel that having a bit of an advance warning would be nice—if you know ahead of time, you may be able to turn around and go in a different direction or at least slow down.

For most of us, its unpredictability and suddenness is the worst aspect of anger. Like an exploding bomb, anger often leaves behind wreckage, and wandering around the ruins afterward is not very pleasant. Also like an exploding bomb, the damage is done in an instant, whereas repairs may take longer and sometimes are not wholly successful. As my mindfulness practice took hold, my own periods without anger grew longer. I also experienced the capacity of mindfulness to create more self-awareness so that I was aware of the first signs of anger, before it became an unstoppable force. This forewarning capacity of mindfulness has been observed in other emotion-related challenges like depression. It happens as a by-product of a regular mindfulness practice.

Finding a Rainbow of Feelings Inside Anger

At its origin, anger has a healthy core, as it is a reaction to unmet needs.

"Many children ago, my wife, Martha, and I noticed that the more we carried our babies, the less they cried. So when child number six, Mathew, was born, Martha made a sling from an old bedsheet to carry him around. She loved 'wearing' Mathew. The sling was like a piece of clothing—she put it on in the morning and took it off in the evening. And with that, the term 'babywearing' was born in the Sears household," recounts Dr. William Sears, a pediatrician, in *The Baby Book*. Indeed, when traveling in Guatemala myself, I did not hear any crying babies in the crowded "chicken buses," in the narrow streets of native pueblos, or anywhere else. This is not because Mayan babies are missing the "crying gene," but rather because Mayan mothers wear their babies and are sensitive to the baby's every move. They take care of the needs of the baby before it starts crying.

Crying is a sign of frustration; the baby signals its need by fussing first. If that gets no response, it starts to whimper. If that gets no response, it starts to cry, then to howl in fury. Perhaps in households where they are not worn, babies have learned to skip the first few steps because they produce no effect, or perhaps mothers are not there to notice those few steps and think that the baby goes directly from contentment to howling.

When needs are not met, there is first sadness, then frustration, then anger. This has led Dr. Marshall Rosenberg, the creator of Nonviolent Communication, to look at anger as a secondary emotion. It is secondary not in importance but in a temporal sequence—there is first a need that is not being met, then feelings of sadness or disappointment because of that unmet need, then anger.

Imagine a scenario where John is angry when he discovers that his spouse, Martha, has been cheating on him. Behind John's anger, there is his need to trust a person who is so close to him, and disappointment and sadness that Martha has betrayed that trust. And behind that, there is his love for her. In the heat of his anger, John might be quite unaware of his original needs and of his feelings of disappointment and sadness.

The essence of Nonviolent Communication is to be able to feel and express the original feelings that led to the anger. In John's case, the original feelings were love and trust. Then came disappointment and sadness. These can be expressed in nonviolent ways, in ways that elicit understanding and sympathy, whereas anger is often expressed as revenge, as name-calling, or in other violent ways that call forth negative reactions.

When you feel anger, ask yourself what need was frustrated.

Get in touch with the feelings of sadness or disappointment that came up. Those are the real causes of anger. You can feel waves of revenge-seeking thoughts well up inside you. But can you also feel the original sadness or disappointment, and the original need that was quite legitimate and understandable? Can you express those needs instead of "diagnosing" the other person with negative words? This is the key to communicating in a nonviolent way.

Our needs fuel other emotions as well. If you are feeling anxious, for example, ask yourself what needs are behind your anxiety. Is it a need for safety? Is it a need for connection—do you feel that your love need is being threatened? Or perhaps your need to feel competent?

As you get in touch with your needs, you have a better chance of dealing with them rationally.

9

NEED VS. GREED

When you are discontent, you always want more, more, more. Your desire can never be satisfied. But when you practice contentment, you can say to yourself, "Oh yes—I already have everything that I really need."

—THE DALAI LAMA

I decide to take a break, stroll over to the park, and sit on a bench. Suddenly, a myriad of sensations engage my senses: The spring sun penetrates deep and warms up my bones, a light breeze caresses my skin, and the rich texture of green leaves on trees is infinitely more interesting to my eye than the monotonous paint on the walls of my home. Here, as I sit in the sun, I surrender to the pleasant feelings I'm experiencing, and I feel that if I were a cat, I would soon start purring.

Contentment is grounded in the body—we feel contentment in our senses and in our guts, literally, as a meal can be a gateway to contentment. As our stomach fills, we secrete leptin and other satiety hormones. During sexual intimacy, we secrete oxytocin, which brings feelings of happiness and contentment. With need, there is a natural mechanism that signals when the need has been satisfied.

There are no such hormones of contentment with greed. On the contrary, greed satisfaction may be stimulating addiction pathways that keep pressing us for more, as in gambling. As a result, our craving is further stimulated. We can feel contentment when our needs are met, which are relatively few in number. But focusing on our wants can bring discontent, because our wants can be numerous or even unlimited.

When wants are disconnected from needs, they lose their power to satisfy even when they are gratified, for we are satisfied only when our needs are satisfied. Satisfying our need for food and drink brings contentment. But we can eat and drink only a limited amount before discomfort sets in. Trying to gratify greed for food that is disconnected from need will bring bloating, indigestion, and eventually weight gain and even obesity. Obesity brings a trail of other health challenges and steals years from our life span.

Do you think King Solomon's wish to have one thousand wives was connected to his needs, or do you think that he lost touch with his needs and started following his greed? Did having all those women bring him contentment?

Here is the story of one of them, a woman named Abishag. Solomon's older brother Adonijah took a fancy to Abishag and asked their mother, Bathsheba, to intercede for him so that he could have her. Solomon responded by having his brother put to death. Perhaps he had forgotten the commandment "Thou shalt not kill."

Nor is this the end of this sordid story. Solomon then exiled his father David's priest Abiathar because he had sided with Adonijah in this family squabble. This much made its way to the Bible. My hunch is that it is the tip of the iceberg, and more unhappiness followed this one wife's trail. Murdering your brother creates waves that reverberate through the family. It may ruin your relationship with your nieces and nephews. It may strain your relationship with your mother. And keep in mind that there were 999 other wives, each with their own lives and connections. These women were not just numbers.

Here's another story of greed closer to my home. Nicolas is a jack-of-all-trades who has done occasional odd jobs for me in his spare time. He works full time for a wealthy businessman who owns a vast mansion in a posh section of town. Nicolas told me that his boss was having some troubles recently. He had bought a seventh luxury car, but there was space for only six in his garage. So he took down the old garage and part of the house and built a bigger garage. But the new construction did not pass the city's inspection—the construction had exceeded the building permit he had obtained. Nicolas's boss was now faced with some unpleasant choices as a result of following his greed.

YOU CAN'T ALWAYS GET WHAT YOU WANT

"You get what you need," the Rolling Stones song says. It helps to be clear about the difference between our needs and our wants. Solomon needed one wife but wanted a thousand of them. Here's the thinking behind the happiness paradox: Since one wife makes me so happy, two will make me twice as happy. Since one plate of spaghetti makes me feel so good, two will make me feel twice as good.

There is a sense of the tragic in this train of thought, because it is fueled by a kind of innocence—the innocence of a child. Our eyes are bigger than our stomachs, bigger than the matrimonial bed, and even bigger than the garage. Can we come back and reconnect with all the sensations in the stomach—the sensation of satiety as well as the sensation of hunger? Can we come back and reconnect with the emotional intimacy and the shared happiness of a couple? And can we come back and reconnect with our need for transportation and the car as a means to that end? Need is closer to the body, whereas greed is closer to the mind. Can we come back from being in the mind and in our thoughts to being with our feelings and sensations in the body?

Stop feeding greed. The feeling of satiety comes from the body, but greed comes from the mind. The greedy person lives more in her mind than in her body. It may not seem obvious, but the cure for greed starts with getting in touch and staying in touch with the body.

MEDITATION AND THE PRACTICE OF HAPPINESS

According to neuroscientists, meditation activates the left prefrontal region of the brain, the same region that is activated when we smile. It can bring us contentment. Look at contentment as a purring cat—its needs have been met, and it is happy. Perhaps that is why cats can find contentment more easily than humans. They are closer to their bodies. The mindfulness agenda of coming back to our home in the body is also a prerequisite for contentment and happiness. So is the practice of being here, now: A discontented child could be crying while sitting among a pile of toys, because she wants the one thing that isn't there—she wants the thing that is in her mind. A contented child is willing to engage with what *is* there.

DOES GREED HAVE A MALE FACE?

I cannot help noticing that the desire for cars and women in the preceding examples are typical male traits. Is it only a coincidence that they came to mind first when I was looking for instances of outstanding greed? It has indeed been remarked that men are in general greedier than women—they are twice as likely to be addicted to gambling and to drugs, for example. Men hankering for bonuses and promotions were the driving force behind the recent banking meltdown, and more men than women are obese. A craving for power drives politicians, who are predominantly male, and there is only one woman among the ten richest people on the planet. Has there ever been a woman with a thousand husbands? I doubt it. There is much fodder for mindfulness in this area—greed has always been a favorite subject of Buddhist practice.

PRACTICE SONG
"There's Honey in Each Moment"

There's honey in each moment, there's a blessing in each day.
Taste the honey of this moment; touch the blessing of this day.
Make your journey step by step; enjoy the flowers along the way.
There's no end, no escape, there's only a peaceful heart.

Some moments can feel like pure honey, but this mantra does not say that there is *only* honey in each moment. Neither is this song another "Oklahoma!" The honey here is not the prospect of another romance or the exaltation of a beautiful morning. Here, the honey is simply the blessing of being alive and sharing this planet, our home, with other beings. In this sense, the honey is always there as long as we are alive, even when everything is not going our way, and even when there are other tastes such as hot peppers on the spice shelf of life.

We often take the honey for granted. We are distracted by the business of living and do not pay attention to the honey till only a few drops are left in the jar. Then the sweetness of life hits us with full force. When we are young, we may think that there is an endless supply of sweet days ahead of us and that life is nothing special. Cancer survivors know better. They have faced their mortality and emerged the wiser. But you do not have to get cancer to acquire this wisdom. Open up to the sweetness and the blessing of each day, to the possibilities it offers.

We receive the gift of life, a twenty-four-hour gift coupon, every day. What do we do with this gift?

We can practice waking up to the gift of each day with appreciation. Waking up physically is one thing—waking up to the blessing of the day is another. Do both each morning.

The last line of the song points out that each morning you will wake up to the same body, the same brain, the same job, the same house, and the same world. There is no escape from this. Of course, you can make a change somewhere, but then you will wake up to that changed situation every morning from then on.

You can do it with a peaceful heart, with acceptance and serenity, or you can do it with a struggle. The choice is yours.

10

GETTING OUT OF THE BOX OF YOURSELF

> *People have a hard time letting go of their*
> *suffering. Out of a fear of the unknown, they*
> *prefer suffering that is familiar.*
> —THICH NHAT HANH
>
> *The greatest habit you can ever break*
> *is the habit of being yourself.*
> —JOE DISPENZA

Sally is tense. I can feel the tension as I approach her. She is also a master of one-upmanship—whatever I say, she will come back with a retort that shows she is smarter. In her late forties, Sally has had few lasting relationships, although she is attractive and is successful in her career. She also has a sense of humor that I enjoy, even though it is sometimes directed at me. She lives alone.

Tall and fiftyish, David is sad looking and rarely smiles. He also lives alone. When I visit and chat, I laugh in my usual casual manner, and I sometimes feel out of place, as if I went to a funeral and cracked jokes to make people laugh.

Sally and David are addicted to their own personalities even though they flirt with change. David meditates every day. Sally reads self-help books and attends personal growth workshops. But they do not change even though they feel a certain limitation in their personal lives. They cling to their mental habits and to their default mental states—this is home ground for them: They would feel like they were not being themselves if they were to act differently. A fun-loving person feels somewhat frivolous to David. A peaceful person feels a bit strange to Sally.

MEDITATING INSIDE THE BOX

Einstein once said, "We can't solve problems by using the same kind of thinking we used when we created them." I assume he was talking about problems in physics, but what he is saying is also true about meditation and change.

You are the box. In this box there is furniture from long ago, from the dark reaches of evolution, from the time you spent in your parents' house, and from the redbrick (or gray concrete) schoolhouse you attended, and the boys and girls with whom you shared good and bad times. When you think, your mind is used to going around this furniture. Like the candle that does not illuminate its own shadow, you may not see your own blind spots, for your blind spots are part of the box you are in—whether it is the sadness box, the stress box, or the box you see as your self, with your habits and biases. Meditating inside a box makes you become aware of the box—and meditation practice primarily is about coming out of the box.

Our attitude and worldview tend to become entrenched. At some level we may wish to be less anxious or happier, yet at another level, we may cling to our old habits and attitudes. There is safety in familiarity. We may even look at people who do not share our anxiety or sadness as somehow deficient.

A MEDITATING MOSQUITO?

A mosquito was keeping me company as I tried to write this chapter. I was sitting on the patio, and at one time it sat with me while taking a break from circling my arms. I tried to imagine it in meditation. Assuming that it tried, do you think that as a result of its meditation this insect would have a change of heart and decide to stop biting people? Wouldn't it be more likely to sit daydreaming about soft skin and tasty blood?

Some people sit like the mosquito, and their meditation confirms their old habits instead of changing them. This may be because that is all they know. It may also be because they have chosen the wrong model of practice—there are many different types of meditation, some of which chase after unclear or esoteric goals. Maharishi Mahesh Yogi comes to mind; he is the one who inspired the Beatles—remember "The Fool on the Hill"?

Day after day, alone on the hill
The man with the foolish grin is keeping perfectly still . . .

Unfortunately, soon after his encounter with the Beatles, Maharishi started teaching levitation as the purpose of meditation practice.

Here's what I'd like to know: If a measly mosquito can levitate, why spend so much effort trying to learn how to do it? Aren't there more important things in life than trying to imitate a mosquito?

MINDFULNESS MEDITATION

When you are looking for meditation instruction, choose a *mindfulness meditation* group or retreat. Groups connected with Thich Nhat Hanh, Vipassana, or Insight Meditation aim to simplify your life instead of complicating it, and they aim to reduce stress and lead the way toward peace of mind and insight.

Another suggestion: It is a good idea not to isolate yourself in your practice. A teacher or meditation coach can direct you toward more helpful ways of meditating. Practicing with a group may also help if there is time set aside for sharing. In such a group, you may learn from others, and they may learn from you.

CLEAR THE DESK

Imagine you are an accountant. A client is just leaving, and your desktop is cluttered with her papers—tax forms, receipts, and invoices. Before you greet your next client, you need to clear your desk; otherwise there will be confusion—the new client's papers will be mixed up with the papers on your desk. Sounds like an obvious thing to do, and most accountants do it routinely—yet one must also clear the mind so that one is free and available for what comes next, and that is not always done. For six years in a row, my accountant missed an important tax deduction that I was entitled to. I know that she is very competent and has some big accounts. My only explanation is that her attention was not wholly focused on my case.

"Clearing the desk" mentally is even more important after an event that involves the emotions, such as an altercation at work or a family discussion. Retreats and periods of formal meditation prepare you for this, because they give you some experience in emptying the mind and freeing the heart. You must now do this contextually—you must do in a few minutes what you practiced during a whole retreat, and you must do it more than once a day. The world of work does not always allow time for this—if you are a schoolteacher, a new group of kids arrives with the bell whether you are ready for them or not. But "clearing the desk" is a necessity for smooth functioning, as much in the context of work as in our personal lives. We must make room for the next event somehow. Here is a poem that points the way:

Children's castles, lovers' footprints, the agony of drying starfish,
all gone

as the surf wipes clean the beach
with fresh waves coming from the vastness of the ocean.

Let the breath wipe away yesterday's words,
the morning's thoughts,
and the tightness that remains of them,
until there is only this moment's freshness. (J. E.)

In a recent group, one participant shared that when she came home from work, she always took a few breaths in front of the door to compose herself, find her freshness, and let go of the stress of work. She did not want to burden her husband and children with her own stress. When she entered the house, she was open, receptive, and ready to listen to others. Another participant was listening intently: "I do the exact opposite," he confessed with some regret. "I come home and lay all my burdens onto my wife, and it distresses her." I could tell that he had glimpsed something. I hoped that he would remember this conversation as he returned from work the next day.

This subject had come up before, and a previous participant had made us a present of a brown paper bag on which she had written, *STRESS BAG: THROW ALL YOUR PROBLEMS INSIDE* with a marker. A bag like that, sitting by the entrance, can be a good reminder.

BECOMING AWARE OF THE BOX

Many of the people who attend my classes are there because they have become aware of the box they are in and are starting to feel limited by it. This may have happened because of a loss or crisis, a burnout, a breakup, or by coming across a book or an Internet site that hints at the promise of a more satisfying life. But even though they want to change, sometimes at another level they still want to stay the same. They are addicted to themselves, and even though they may look wistfully at a freer, less stressed life, they also want to preserve their old familiar habits and attitudes. They want to change and stay the same all at the same time.

LETTING GO

The parable of the monkey with her hand in a jar of peanuts is a telling one. The mouth of the jar is just wide enough for the monkey to get her hand in. But once she makes a fist holding the peanuts, she can't get her hand out, and she is caught because she can't let go of the peanuts in her fist.

I have my own version of that story: When I was water-skiing for the first time, I fell but continued to hang on to the rope. As the boat dragged me through the water, I noticed that my bathing shorts had slipped down to my ankles.

I understand how that monkey felt.

It is not always easy to let go of the rope, to let go of the past, to let go of who you believe you are, or to let go of a relationship that does not bring you happiness.

Visualizing a life without holding on can help: If you can visualize something, you are one step closer to doing it.

VISUALIZE THE CHANGE

If we want to have a relationship with someone and we already see ourselves doing it, then we ask him or her out. If we find it difficult to visualize the possibility, we may not "see ourselves doing it" and we do not ask.

This comes naturally to some people—they visualize romantic encounters with every attractive man or woman they see. Those are the people who have no difficulty getting dates. Successful businesspeople have the same knack with starting an enterprise—they see possibilities everywhere and find it easy to see themselves in business.

Visualizing is not magic, though—it is only a step toward action. John Lennon's song "Imagine" may now give us the impression that just imagining peace is all we need to do. But Lennon did not stop with imagining—he was actively working for peace. At one point, President Nixon tried to have him deported because he feared that Lennon's antiwar efforts might interfere with his reelection chances. Even "just" writing peace songs and promoting them is a form of activism. If you think it is easy, try doing it.

WHO IS CHANGING?

We all have the ability to change the direction of our lives. But if we identify too strongly with our habits, attitudes, views, default states of mind, circumstances, or occupation, change may feel strange. We may feel that by changing, we are being disloyal to ourselves, to who we are. But such a feeling may also lead us to loyalty to our stress, our anxiety, or our sadness. In a poem titled "Only Breath," Rumi considers various cultural, religious, and biological identities that may define him, and he rejects them all. He finally comes to the conclusion that:

"I am a breath breathing human."

By staying with the breath continually, you *become* Rumi's "breath breathing human." Then, no matter how much you change the circumstances and conditions of your life, you still remain yourself in an essential way, because *that* is who you really are.

MEDITATION COACHING

Private interviews with a teacher are a big help in curing self-addiction. In the Zen tradition, they are called *Dokusan*. In a retreat featuring all-day sittings, they are offered several times a day. They are also offered, albeit less often, in a ten-day Vipassana retreat. Private interviews are available in the retreats Thich Nhat Hanh gives. In these retreats, there are usually several monastic and lay Dharma teach-ers in attendance. Inquire and find the person who makes the schedule. In addi-tion, every Thich Nhat Hanh retreat features a session of questions and answers where Thich Nhat Hanh himself takes questions from the retreatants. Such en-counters help move your practice forward.

COUPLES COUNSELING

The mind can hold opposing attitudes—unconscious attitudes, perhaps devel-oped during childhood, can exist side by side with other attitudes that we hold consciously. Those unconscious attitudes can still drive our behavior. There are instances of well-to-do people who steal and poor people who are generous, of priests who are child molesters and family men who are rapists, of depressed co-medians and unhinged psychotherapists.

When someone, let's call her Linda, comes to my stress-reduction class, I often see two people at the door, and it is not because I have double vision:

1. Linda, the one complaining about her stress; and
2. Linda's stress; I'll call her Glinda in honor of the Good Witch in *The Wizard of Oz.*

The two personalities become very clear as soon as Linda, the spokeswoman for both, starts to talk. Linda would like to be less stressed, but Glinda won't let her. Glinda hides behind the furniture in Linda's mind—behind her ideas and opinions—and plays hide-and-seek with Linda. Glinda is also a person in some ways—she borrows Linda's body and mind. Stress is in the body, and stress is also in the mind. The unfortunate thing is that Linda and Glinda do not communicate well. Otherwise, my services would be unnecessary, and they would not be here. The situation is a bit like couples counseling.

"How is this possible?" you might think. "Aren't there one hundred trillion connections in the human brain? It is a pretty straightforward situation: Linda wants to be more relaxed. How come she does not seem to be able to get that message across to the rest of her body and brain? What happened to the much-vaunted connectivity of the brain? Why does she need you to be the go-between?"

CONNECTED BUT NOT COMMUNICATING

I would like to open a parenthesis here and suggest that connectivity might not be the same thing as communication. Studies indicate that with a placebo, a person with depression can produce more serotonin, and a person who has Parkinson's disease can produce more dopamine. Yet the person is unable to tell her brain directly to produce more of these substances—the needed communication does not happen even though the connections are there. The doctor and her placebo are somehow necessary to initiate the communication between different parts of the brain.

Back to Linda and her witch. At first sight, it looks like Glinda is the problem: She is uncooperative, she is unruly, and she is not listening to Linda, even as Linda pleads with her in obvious distress.

Yet if Glinda could speak, she might say something like, "I do not understand Linda. What does 'more relaxed' actually mean? What does Linda want me to do specifically? She is not telling me the details. She is speaking only in generalities and abstractions. This is sad, because when Linda is unhappy, I'm unhappy too." So they end up in couples counseling, and as Linda is the one who made the appointment, I listen to her, but my sympathies are with Glinda—she is the misunderstood one.

"We are one," says a New Age song. Yet experience shows that sometimes, even one of us is not always "one," and even one of us can be a "we." A good part of stress is in the body, but the body is often unable to make itself heard and understood. The body speaks in sensations, not in words. But many of us are in our heads most of the time and not focused on bodily sensations; we are busy thinking words. So, just like a couple who goes for counseling, as Linda complains that Glinda does not listen to her, Glinda also feels that Linda is not listening to her. Body Scan–type meditations are useful, because they initiate a situation in which the meditator is driven to listen to her body. You can find a number of Body Scan meditations on YouTube.

In this book, both sides of a person are addressed. You will find much material here addressing the side that holds our beliefs and attitudes. That is because they are the furniture of the mind, and just as we go around the furniture when we walk in our living room, we are constantly going around our beliefs and attitudes as we think. If we want to be more comfortable in our living room, we may need to get rid of some old furniture.

At the same time, thinking itself—especially overthinking—is also a problem. The practice materials such as guided meditations and practice themes, songs,

PRACTICE THEME
Surrender to Your Breath

Surrender to your breath,
Surrender to your breath,
Surrender to your breath each moment.
Surrender to your love,
Surrender to your love,
Surrender to your love each moment.
Surrender all your stress,
Surrender all your stress,
Surrender all your stress each moment.

and poems are meant to calm the mind and lead us toward a different kind of thinking—"thinking without thoughts," as the Dalai Lama once put it.

Who is surrendering? The conscious, thinking, obsessing, ruminating mind that thinks it is in charge of the world. The mind, the brain, the controller, the self-important one. Maybe also the one who is anxious and believes that her anxiety is what is holding the world together.

This is just another way of saying, "Focus on the breath," but with a nuance. For what is preventing us from focusing on the breath? The thinking brain that has a choke hold on us and does not want to yield its grip. This song points a flashlight at it and asks it specifically to relent.

Why is this a problem? Because the conscious mind makes such important decisions as buying a house and getting married, and also many professional decisions such as who should go to prison and for how long, or who needs a heart replacement, and it feels important and in charge. And what does the unconscious mind do? Not much of importance, according to the conscious mind: just ordinary things like breathing, digesting food, and going to the bathroom.

Ignoring it and turning our attention to the breath can feel like a slap in the face to the conscious mind—after all, we spent many years in school developing the competencies of this mind. We worked hard in honing its skills during our career, and we are proud of its accomplishments. For many of us, it is who we are. In a way, this meditation is asking us to give up who we think we are.

But look closer and you will see that this meditation theme is actually trying to enlarge our narrow vision of who we think we are. It is trying to incorporate the breathing, and all else that comes with it, into our notion of self.

This is the beginning of wisdom.

PRACTICE POEM

Read this short text and the poem before sitting for meditation. Then let the auditory and visual image of waves on a beach guide the rhythm of your breathing. Breathe rhythmically like waves spreading on a sandy beach and hear the waves as you breathe. Stay with this visualization for the first few minutes of your meditation period or until you are comfortably focused on your breath.

For the second part of your meditation period, you can continue enjoying your rhythmic breathing and breathe with the many creatures that came before us—wave upon wave of beings who came and went before us.

At some point, just let go of all visualizations.

"The Beach"

Waves come in and go out
with the slow, majestic rhythm of a giant breathing.
They shuffle the shells on the beach
and slowly grind them down.
Each shell particle on this golden sand
once had bright eyes,
felt hunger, fear,
and satisfaction like me.
With each coming wave
they still hiss and murmur
stories about beautiful lives
waves and waves ago.
For beauty is in nature,
the nature of each shell creature
my nature, your nature,
shining under the bright sun. (J. E.)

11

SELF-REGULATION

*Feelings come and go like clouds
in a windy sky.
Conscious breathing is my anchor.*

—THICH NHAT HANH

We self-regulate all the time. We regulate our body temperature, blood pressure, the cadence of our heartbeat, and myriad other biological functions all day and all night. The capacity for self-regulation is essential for life, and when we lose that capacity, we die. We are also self-regulating when we can sleep when we need to, get out of bed when we need to, and relax when we want to. We are self-regulating when we can stop eating when we are full.

You will notice that this list started out with functions that we consider purely biological and is now getting into areas that are influenced by emotions. Indeed, emotional self-regulation is a skill we first learn as children. We learn it as babies through our attachment to our mother—as our mother soothes us with her positive emotions when we feel discomfort and cry, we gradually learn to soothe ourselves with positive emotions following her example. Biological and emotional self-regulation are related—the heart rate and blood pressure of a crying baby also turn toward normal as she is soothed. This connection is at the heart of how emotional self-regulation can strengthen our immunity, improve our health, and lengthen our life spans—when we are infused with positive emotions and feel good, our body also reaps the benefits.

SELF-CONTROL OR SELF-REGULATION?

When an upset and crying baby is soothed and she stops crying, she is not exercising self-control. It is not the case that she still feels upset but is refraining from crying through self-control. Rather, she has been influenced by the positive emotions of her mother, by her loving touch and calm voice, and the emotional storm has abated now, the sun is out, and the birds are chirping—the baby is smiling and cooing.

When we exercise self-control, we may still be angry, but we do not strike out; or we refrain from saying mean things. We are nevertheless like a bomb ready to go off—the anger is still there. It's a hair-trigger situation. One more drop can overcome our self-control any time—we all have our limits.

When we self-regulate, on the other hand, anger has been replaced by equanimity, positive emotions have taken hold, and self-control is not necessary, for there is no storm. The weather service reports sunny skies.

Self-control is linked with repression, and self-regulation with a measure of equanimity. Self-control is needed when equanimity is lacking.

We achieve self-control by biting our lips. We can move toward equanimity and self-regulation with mindfulness meditation. Most of the time, we practice a mix of the two, but the closer the mix is to self-regulation, the more comfortable it feels.

AWAKENING OR SELF-REGULATION?

I used to think that in the days of old, people took up a spiritual path such as Buddhism to get wisdom and become enlightened. I thought that only in our day did mindfulness teachings became an important tool in the arsenal of psychologists for helping people with their personal problems, their stress and depression. I was wrong. In Buddha's time as in ours, people took up meditation for their own reasons, sometimes to obtain wisdom, but sometimes also to achieve better self-regulation, just as they do now.

Here are a couple of stories from that time. Bhadda Kundalakesa was a young woman from a wealthy family who married a man of questionable character out of love. Sometime later, he took her to a mountaintop with the purpose of pushing her to her death down a rocky cliff. He wanted to get his hands on her money and her jewels. A scuffle ensued, and she ended up by pushing him down the cliff instead. She was understandably distraught by what happened and started wandering about in a state of confusion and desolation until she encountered a disciple of the Buddha and, through him, the Buddha himself. She obtained peace and equanimity as a result of that encounter.

In my previous book *Buddha's Book of Stress Reduction*, I recounted the story of another woman who became distressed as a result of what we would call a "crib death" today—she woke up to find her baby son lifeless next to her. Kisa Gotami also found solace in her encounter with the Buddha.

In fact, mindfulness, wisdom, and self-regulation are all related, and there is no wisdom without self-regulation.

"THE RIDDLE SONG"

Suffering is a part of life, and it starts early.

Babies are usually born crying and not laughing, and they go on from there. "The Riddle Song" plays with this idea:

I gave my love a cherry without a stone
I gave my love a chicken without a bone
I gave my love a ring that had no end
I gave my love a baby with no crying.

Puzzled? The song expects you to be, and continues with:

How can there be a baby with no crying?

And gives the solution in the last line:

A baby when it's sleeping, has no crying.

What about adults? Are we also contented only during our sleeping hours?

We do not express our discontent as often and as loudly as babies do, but there are some signs that we feel it. Statistics say that most people are unhappy at their jobs, and that only seventeen percent of marriages are happy ones. A cynic might point out that the obvious remedy is not to work and not to marry. Alas, there are no statistics on how happy cynics are. . . .

Buddha's wisdom started with the recognition that some kind of discomfort, discontent, or suffering is part of life. It may be acute, as when someone gets a diagnosis of cancer or suffers a loss or the breakup of a relationship. Such events test the limits of our self-regulation skills, sometimes exceeding them. If, as a result, a person tries to kill herself, she is sent to a psychiatrist. If she tries to kill somebody else, she is sent to prison (according to statistics, there are three suicides for every two homicides). But the causes can be the same—overwhelming emotions and a failure to self-regulate. Fortunately, most of us are not in that acute state of suffering. Our suffering may be an underlying sense of discomfort or uneasiness, with friends or family, with work, with not getting enough sleep, with gaining too much weight . . . this book is not long enough to list all our possible complaints.

Our usual reaction to suffering is to try to self-regulate in some way so as to avoid being overwhelmed. Some of our attempts at self-regulation are healthy and give good results. Some others—such as trying to suppress our feelings, self-medicating, or drinking—do not work well, because an important part of self-regulation is awareness of emotions. These "solutions" prevent self-awareness. However, we need awareness in order to come to terms with our emotions and to transform them. Otherwise, they just go underground.

About ten percent of people face another significant challenge in this area. They are the ones who drive their relationship partners up a wall because they do not talk about their feelings—they do not talk about them because they have nothing to say. They are not aware of their feelings. Understandably, they do not take an active part in conversations where others' feelings are discussed. This trait is called *alexithymia*. Despite the common perception that this is an exclusively male club, about a third of alexithymics are women. It is better to look at this ten percent as the people who are at the extreme end of a continuum. We all fall somewhere on this scale, and at the other end are those fiction writers and singers who are virtuosos at describing or expressing their emotions.

My experience confirms that mindfulness meditation widens our emotional scale. When I was a young music student, I wrote many dissonant pieces of music—it seemed like the thing to do. It was all very abstract, without any discernible feeling. Students in the music departments of many universities still churn out this kind of music "like farmers produce surplus corn," as Igor Stravinsky once put it. Could this have something to do with an inability to feel and express the full gamut, the full richness of human emotions? As you listen to my practice songs, you may notice that now I have a wide range of expression.

I also went through the "I cannot sing" phase for a while. I was always looking for singers who could express in their voice the feelings that I felt unable to express myself. But as I began to experience my own feelings more strongly, the urge to express them by singing became stronger. I worked at this until I felt capable of doing it. What you hear now is the result.

Emotions happen in the body. If we see a car speeding toward us out of nowhere, our body reacts physically—we slam on the brakes or swerve. As the brain reads our bodily signals, such as a higher heart rate, increased muscle tension, and higher blood pressure, it creates the feeling of fear. Feeling is the subjective experience of an emotion. The emotion happens anyway, whether we feel it or not.

Brain scientist Joseph LeDoux, in *The Emotional Brain*, writes that "connections from the emotional systems to the cognitive systems are stronger than connections from the cognitive systems to the emotional systems." The result is that "while conscious control over emotions is weak, emotions can flood consciousness."

This is another challenge to emotional self-control—we all start with an anatomical handicap. This makes cultivating equanimity with mindfulness meditation all the more necessary.

Despite its etymology (*e* + *motion*), sometimes emotion can also keep us from moving forward. Seething anger or jealousy can eat up all our energy—energy that should be focused on our goals and values. While we are renewing our anger with thoughts like "How could she do that to me?" and fantasizing about how best to punish the offender, our life stalls. While we are stewing in fear about a dreaded outcome, opportunities are continually coming and going all around us—opportunities we are too busy to appreciate. While self-pity saps all our energy, it is hard to live up to our full potential. When emotions take over the mind, we are revving the engine in neutral, and despite much noise and smoke, we are going nowhere.

Self-regulation makes it possible to move forward smoothly.

MINDFULNESS AND FLOW

Thoughts, feelings, and mental states are meant to flow, because they are responses to events. As events change, our responses consisting of thoughts, feelings, and mental states also need to change if they are to keep up with what is happening. When we hang on to an emotion, when we wear a sad face to a party, this is like continuing to wear a raincoat after the rain has stopped and the sun is shining. It is like wearing snow boots around the house after you come in on a snowy day. It is like wearing pajamas to work.

When we hang on to sadness after a distressing event or a distressing thought comes and goes, we stop the flow. Our state of mind becomes calcified and turns into depression. Like a stalled clock that shows the right time only twice a day, it is inappropriate most of the time.

When we hang on to a fleeting moment of worry about tomorrow's presentation, it becomes anxiety. The fleeting moment of worry may have been justified. It was meant to motivate us to review the presentation. After the review, it is time for another state of mind—an appropriate one may be satisfaction or confidence. When our emotional flow gets dammed, the anxiety persists, even though now it is no longer appropriate. Instead of motivating us toward the right action (the review), it now gets in the way. It may make us nervous during the presentation; it may make us choke.

Sometimes, feelings come and refuse to leave. The outside conditions change, but our feelings do not. Then we get emotionally stuck—we are still living in a past moment and reacting to past circumstances. "Feelings come and go like clouds in a windy sky" describes the state of affairs in a flexible heart. Sometimes an oppressive dark cloud of smog covers the sky for weeks and weeks.

"Clear the desk." Get rid of the emotional clutter. Respond, instead of hanging on. Being in the moment also means responding to the moment. Be mindful of lagging behind—what is causing you to do that? Why are certain terrains like a bog for you?

Mindfulness means being present to the outside world, to events as they happen, but it also means being present to yourself—in this case to feelings that do not keep up with events, to clouds that do not move with the wind. What is holding them back?

Self-regulation is also allowing feelings to come and go without wanting to cling to them or wanting to push them away. Just accepting them, making friends with them, soothing them if necessary. And then going on with life, doing what needs to be done, doing one's best. Responding to circumstances openly and with compassion.

Seeing clearly what each moment demands, taking a deep breath, and rising to the occasion to the best of one's ability.

Attitudes That Imprison Us

For centuries, people believed that gods and goddesses determined the course of their lives—their successes as well as their failures. When you read Homer describing the war of Troy or the adventures of Odysseus, you get a glimpse of this belief at work. The *Iliad* begins by stating that the cause of the pestilence that struck the Greek army on its way to Troy was the anger of the god Apollo with Agamemnon, their king. De-responsibilizing attitudes such as these are also common in medicine today. Many doctors believe that cholesterol is the cause of heart disease, not faulty diet or lack of exercise, and chemical imbalance is the cause of depression and anxiety—not emotional imbalance and faulty thinking habits. The individual is not empowered by such beliefs.

Attitudes That Empower Us

With mindfulness we take responsibility for our acts, both our overt acts of doing and the covert acts of thinking. This happens as mindfulness fosters awareness of what we are doing. We have to become aware of what we are doing before we can change it. By changing what we can—what is directly in our control—we also indirectly change our states of mind, our moods, and the state of our health, for these depend to a large extent on our behavior and our thinking.

SELF-REGULATING WITH ALCOHOL?

It is ironic that we sometimes drink in an attempt to self-regulate—to feel better, to "forget our troubles," or to loosen up. However, alcohol is a substance that puts us at a handicap and actually reduces our power to self-regulate.

Why is it not legal to drink and drive? Because alcohol interferes with our self-regulation skills—physically as well as emotionally, as many drunk drivers get lost in the euphoria of driving fast and get into accidents. According to a World Health

Organization (WHO) report, alcohol consumption killed 3.3 million people world-wide in 2012.

More effective ways of self-regulation are discussed in this chapter and through-out this book. "If every eight-year-old in the world is taught meditation, we will eliminate violence from the world within one generation," the Dalai Lama once said, pointing the way.

GETTING CARRIED AWAY

Here is another story from Greek mythology: Daedalus was a master craftsman who lived with his son Icarus on the Greek island of Crete. At one time, Daedalus fell out with Minos, the ruler of Crete, and was imprisoned in the labyrinth that he himself had constructed some time ago. But there was no holding him back. He made two pairs of wings out of bird feathers held together with wax, one for him-self, and one for his son, and they took off together. But Icarus, being young, be-came giddy with his new powers of flight. He flew higher and higher and closer and closer to the sun, until the heat of the sun melted the wax that held the feath-ers in his wings together. Icarus came crashing down, plunged into the sea, and drowned.

I see this as a story about failure to self-regulate, for it is not only the negative mental states of anxiety and depression that create problems when we get car-ried away with them but also excitement and elation. We may get carried away with a drug high and take larger and larger doses, or we may get high from driving fast and get into an accident. Deaths from opioid overdose and from traffic accidents run neck and neck in the United States.

We can also easily get giddy pursuing wealth and power. Buddhist practice stresses the importance of being mindful of all mental states, positive as well as negative.

WISE EMOTION

"Not acting emotionally" does not mean acting without emotion. It means feeling the emotion, whether it is anger, jealousy, or impatience, but not being compelled by it to the point of forgetting one's values, one's compassion, or even one's own benefit in preserving valuable relationships. It means doing what the situation demands rather than what our emotions are pushing us to do.

There is "motion" in "emotion"—fear makes us run from the grizzly in order to save our lives. But in many cases, the "motion" that the emotion pushes us toward is not to our benefit. Anger pushes us to punish the person who made us angry. It may make us say unkind things, which we later regret. Envy pushes us to act in petty ways. And fear can make our careers or relationships stall as we avoid taking an important step out of a vague feeling of apprehension. Even when faced with a grizzly, self-regulation helps—wildlife experts suggest that it may be better to continue facing the beast while retreating backward.

THE CHALLENGE OF FEAR

Emotion is a kind of intelligence—animals live by it and survive. Yet the same fear that helps them escape a predator can sometimes get in the way. I enjoy feeding ducks by the river. I cannot help noticing that some ducks come closer and sometimes even eat out of my hand. They have fear—I can see it in their staccato movements and in their eyes—but they seem to come in spite of their fear, and they get more food than the ducks that stay farther out, watching enviously.

It goes against the grain to feel fear and act bravely. That is why we celebrate heroes—not because they feel no fear, but because they act bravely in spite of their fear, since we all recognize that this is hard to do. Nobody gets a bravery medal for just eating breakfast.

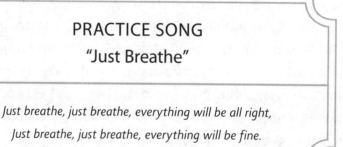

PRACTICE SONG
"Just Breathe"

Just breathe, just breathe, everything will be all right,
Just breathe, just breathe, everything will be fine.

As we improve our self-regulation skills, we can all act in ways that are true to our values, and we can all be more "heroic."

This song came to me when I lost my way while hiking near Sarlat in southwestern France. I had started the hike in the late morning and lingered often to take in the breathtaking views of the Dordogne River from the cliffs along the path. It was already late afternoon by the time I started on my way back. Soon I saw a lovely trail through a thick forest, which seemed to be going in the right direction. I did not resist—I had been walking in the sun all day and welcomed the shade. A few hours later, it was dusk, and I was still walking on an unmarked trail. Soon it started to get seriously dark, and I began to wonder if I was going to be sleeping in my bed or under a tree that night.

At some point along the way, I found myself singing the following words to a simple melody:

Just walk, just walk, everything will be all right,
Just breathe, just breathe, everything will be fine.

What was the alternative? Whatever feelings or thoughts were going through my mind, there was only one thing to do, and that was to keep walking.

Concentrating on the physical sensations of walking and breathing gave my mind something else to do other than worry about getting lost, and I was able to continue walking peacefully, enjoying the magic of being in the deep woods. It also switched my focus from being preoccupied with my destination, which was in the future in any case, to the here-and-now sensations of walking and singing. In the fading light, colors were draining from the scenery around me, and the woods were slowly turning into a black-and-white photograph. When, sometime later, I began to see the lights of the village that I had started from, I greeted them with a smile. Everything *was* indeed fine.

Later, I recognized that this song is a consolation for any kind of worry, not just the worry of getting lost, and I changed the words from "Just walk" to "Just breathe." Since then, it has accompanied me to the dentist's chair for root canal work and to knee surgery. It has kept me company during the intense pain after the anesthetic wore off. It has helped many other people, notably Jenny, a woman in one of my stress-reduction classes. Jenny told me that she was very worried going into radiation therapy after her breast cancer surgery and sang this song to herself on her way into her first session.

In a more general way, this song is also about doing things wholeheartedly. Are you eating? Then just eat. Don't allow yourself to be distracted by other thoughts or by worries. You'll enjoy your meal more that way.

Just eat, just eat, everything will be all right.

Are you driving? Just drive. Taking a shower? Just enjoy the shower.

Center yourself on each breath.

Shift your focus to life that is happening while "you are busy worrying about other things," as John Lennon might have put it.

Worry is about the future—a hypothetical future. Even ordinary pain contains a large percentage of worry.

12

BUDDHA'S GARDEN

*I was born to live
ten thousand lives with
the heart of a child.*

—THICH NHAT HANH

Our inner world is blooming with all kinds of flowering plants—a few that we have planted ourselves but also many that appeared spontaneously. The seeds were there all along in the soil, or they came with the wind, or were brought by birds—there may be thorns of anxiety and the poison ivy of despair growing side by side with the oak tree of stability, dahlias of joy, and violets of love.

A garden is cultivated; we choose the flowers in our garden—at least, we try. This is as true in actual gardens as in our inner gardens. Undesirable weeds seem to appear by themselves, together with desirable plants. But if we do not want thorns and poison ivy, we have to find their roots. Otherwise, they will keep coming out of the ground. We may even be watering them unintentionally if we do not recognize where the roots lie. Again, this is as true of an actual garden as of the metaphoric garden of the heart. Look deeply in the soil of your heart: what are the roots of anxiety and despair? Attitude? Culture? Lifestyle? Your way of thinking? What you habitually read or watch on TV?

If you want dahlias and violets instead of thorns, you need to water them and cultivate them. The more you water and take care of them, the more they will grow. In the metaphoric garden, we water feelings by constantly keeping them in mind. As you think thoughts of love and joy, they will grow in your heart. If you constantly think thoughts of anxiety and despair, those will grow instead. Thorns may grow spontaneously at first, but that is no reason for watering them. You can instead find their roots. You may not be able to take out all the roots—that is why we need to practice mindfulness. But there is no doubt that a garden that is cultivated and well cared for will have fewer weeds and more beneficial plants.

The longer we hold on to a certain feeling, and the more often we come back to it, the stronger it becomes. This is the idea behind the Buddhist metaphor of "watering seeds." The metaphor is rich in implications—seeds lie dormant underground. When we water certain seeds selectively, they can push aboveground and flower. If the seeds in question are undesirable ones, such as the seeds of poison ivy or thorns, it is best not to water them and to let them lie dormant. If, on the other hand, the seeds are desirable ones, we want to water them. We want them to bloom above ground, where we can enjoy their beauty or their beneficial effects.

The Buddha is a gardener. That is what he has been doing for centuries as he sits in meditation in his many images—he has been watering seeds of peace, love, and joy, and his heart has become a delightful garden. As he waters those seeds in his own heart, he simultaneously waters them in the world.

Come and join him in the garden.

PRACTICE SONG
"Buddha's Garden"

Smiling in Buddha's garden, breathing in, breathing out,
Smiling in Buddha's garden, I'm watering flowers of peace.
Smiling in Buddha's garden, breathing in, breathing out,
Smiling in Buddha's garden, I'm watering flowers of love.
Peace grows in the world as it grows in my heart,
Love grows in the world as it grows in my heart,
As peace grows in my heart, it grows in the wide world,
As love grows in my heart, it grows in the world.

Some of us are botanically challenged. We do not know many flowers by name. When we look, we may see a *field* of flowers, or a *garden* of flowers, rather than particular kinds of flowers. The first step in being a good gardener is to know the plants, know the qualities and benefits of each one. Otherwise, we may be weeding out the violets and the irises together with the crabgrass.

The same kind of discrimination is needed for cultivating the garden of the heart.

The first step is recognizing feelings: "There is anger in me," or "There is resentment in me." Are these feelings making you happy? If not, you need to stop rehearsing them. When we cut the crabgrass, it grows back. If we want to get rid of it, we need to get to the root of it. In a way, that is also true of feelings. Ask, "What are the roots of my anger and resentment?" Another person may have triggered these feelings, but the roots are inside you: they are part of your attitude and habits. If you do not get to the roots, the same feelings will keep coming up again and again in similar situations.

This practice song is a bridge between two approaches to meditation. As we look deeply into ourselves and discover the roots of our anxiety, despair, and stress, we are moving from serenity meditation toward insight meditation.

PRACTICE THEME
Create a Buddha Garden

Creating a Buddha garden somewhere in your house is helpful for internalizing it. My Buddha garden has flowers in front of a statue of the Buddha and potted green plants all around. If you do not have a statuette of the Buddha, you can download an image from the Internet or photocopy one from a book. If you are a woman, it may help to have a female figure in your Buddha garden, because the internalized Buddha in your woman's heart will be the same gender as you.

There are lovely images of Quan Yin in books and on the net. Quan Yin is sometimes called the "Female Buddha" in Chinese shops. I have both a Buddha and a Quan Yin in my Buddha garden. My two statues reflect and enjoy each other's mindfulness and positive feelings. As I sit with them, I blend in, so that there are three of us in the garden.

As you practice in your Buddha garden, you also will be inspired to cultivate flowers of positive feelings in the people around you. Take the garden with you when you get up from your meditation. Take it for a walk or a drive. Take it to work. Keep it in your heart when you are with your family or friends. Once you are in touch with the garden in your own heart, you will see other people as walking gardens—for there is a garden in each of us. You can offer people you meet flowers from your garden and enjoy the perfume of the flowers in their hearts. Consider a relationship also as a garden that you cultivate together with your partner; every gesture or word to your partner is like an offering of flowers that enriches your common garden.

GOING DEEPER

There is only one dimension to our lives, and it is both sacred and secular at the same time. We, as well as all living creatures and all natural beings like rivers and mountains, are in that one dimension. It is not that *this* is sacred and *that* is secular. This and that are *both* sacred *and* secular.

A flower contains Earth, wind, and sun—it is a part that contains the whole, defying the laws of logic. In that sense, the flower is sacred, and without end:

The bell:
the universe ringing,

The bird:
the universe singing,
The flower:
the universe blooming. (J. E.)

Such an attitude invites us to do everything reverently and with attention. Mindfulness meditation comes from a tradition that emphasizes the oneness of seemingly separate worlds. Each breath, each step, is taken with that focus. Bringing our mind into alignment with the body is realizing this oneness in practical terms instead of as theory. At least three of the Buddhist precepts—respect for life, mindful sexuality, and abstinence from alcohol—follow from that insight, for violating one of these precepts is violating the sacred nature of the here and the now.

The whole world is a temple, forests are cathedrals, and our bodies are altars. We can feel that as we walk in the deep woods. We can feel it as we hold a baby in our arms or drink from a natural spring on the side of a mountain. These are all occasions for reverence. As we gain intimacy with the sacred dimension of life, we begin to accept it as natural, for it is not only the things that are on the altar that are sacred but all of life. The ordinary is sacred, but the sacred is ordinary as well— it is just everyday life lived with mindfulness.

13

THE PRACTICE OF COMING HOME

> *Mindful breathing*
> *brings you home.*
>
> —THICH NHAT HANH

When Buddha left behind his palatial home at age twenty-nine, he embarked on the homeless life. But "homeless" in this sense also means the opposite of what we usually understand by that word. Buddha gave up having one particular place that he called home, in return for the feeling of being at home in the here-and-now. Now, although he was officially homeless, he was always "at home." In comparison, those of us who are not homeless are away from home most of the day. And if we are not mindful, we are homeless all day. Are you "on your way home" from work, maybe even stuck in traffic? Do not think, "I will soon be home." Think instead, "I have arrived, I am home." These words are sung at Plum Village many times every day—like a constant refrain. Our home is where we are now. Here-and-now is where we always live.

Some blame our runaway technology, our smartphones, and tablet computers for our state of being disconnected from the here-and-now. I'm not so sure. For me, the question is who is in charge: is it the iPhone or I? Is it the computer or I? Television was blamed for all our ills some time ago—before computer addiction there was television addiction. It still persists. Statistics say that Americans still spend five hours a day in front of the TV set. Why? Why does the average person spend nine years of her life watching television? It is a bit simplistic to blame the TV. TV sets do not normally chase people around the house.

OUR HOME IN THE BODY

There are three layers of meaning in the practice of coming home, and they are related. The first is fully inhabiting the here-and-now, as discussed earlier.

Another meaning is coming "home" to the body. If we did not have a body, we really would not have a home! Our stress and our emotions may be caused by our attitudes, but they still manifest in our body. Without body awareness, there is no stress awareness—stress can come and steal our energy and well-being like a thief in the night, and we would not know what happened. In the end, relaxing the body relaxes the mind just as much as relaxing the mind relaxes the body.

In his book *The Face of Emotion*, Dr. Eric Finzi, a dermatologist, tells the story of

Jane, a patient who used to have fights with her husband because when she got annoyed with him (which was often), she frowned. "I didn't even know that it was happening. Then he would ask me if I was mad with him. I tried to deny it, but my face couldn't lie. So he would start to argue, and it went downhill from there." Botox injections fixed all that. Now, she still gets annoyed, but her face doesn't show it, and there are no arguments. They get along much better.

Dr. Finzi goes further. He explains that "the facial expression you make can affect how you *feel*, independent of any social interaction." In a way, "the corpse pose" practiced at the end of many Yoga classes is based on a similar insight—that relaxing the body will relax the mind. This procedure is also used in Body Scan meditation. The insight that the body determines what emotions we feel has a venerable history. William James wrote in 1890 that it is more true to say that "we feel sorry because we cry, angry because we strike, afraid because we tremble," than the other way around. Those of us who belong to the Parents' Club have no doubt observed that sometimes a baby cries because she feels frustrated or angry. But then, as she continues to cry, the crying makes her more frustrated and angrier still.

The brain follows the body, or in Dr. Finzi's words, "Much evidence suggests that our facial expressions are not secondary to, but rather a central driving force of, our emotions." With this as his guiding principle, Dr. Finzi experimented on severely depressed patients by paralyzing their frown muscles with Botox injections. Amazingly, it worked. "Two months after the Botox injection, the majority of patients in the initial trial were no longer clinically depressed by DSM–IV criteria." If you cannot frown, you cannot *feel* sad—without its physical correlate, the emotion does not happen. I should add that facial muscles can get activated even when nothing is happening visibly. The activation is still detectable by electrical measurements on the skin. Try becoming aware of these subliminal twitches as you sit in meditation—the brain thinks with the face muscles as well.

There are many topics of interest in Dr. Finzi's book, including a scientific explanation of Thich Nhat Hanh's saying, "Sometimes I smile because I'm happy, and sometimes I'm happy because I smile." Did you know that if you listen to a joke while holding a pencil between your teeth, you will find it funnier than if you listen to it while holding the pencil between your lips? All because holding the pencil between the teeth mimics a smile, while holding it with your lips mimics a frown.

When we come home to the body, we are fully aware of what is happening in the body. If you came home to your house and found that the kitchen table was upside down, you would notice it. Yet the preceding stories make clear that we are not always "at home" in our bodies—many of us frown without even knowing that we are doing it. We also hold tension and stress in our muscles without being aware of it.

"My shoulders are always tight," complained one participant in a Mindfulness Training class. "I always carry a lot of tension in my shoulders. I have it now." I asked the group to raise their arms, and then went around checking for raised shoulders as I used to do during my ten years as a T'ai Chi teacher. She wasn't the only one with tight shoulders. You do not have to raise your shoulders in order to raise your arms, yet many of us do—we raise our shoulders as we raise the fork to our mouths, as we answer the phone, and as we drive. Low, sloping shoulders used to be seen as a mark of beauty in old times, perhaps because they are signs of a relaxed body and a relaxed mind. Many people look at Sandro Botticelli's *Birth of Venus* and are struck by her beauty. I'm struck by the perfection of her T'ai Chi posture.

Another woman experienced tension in her legs, and a man experienced it in his feet. This is also common—you can check where you usually carry your weight as you stand. Are you carrying more weight on the balls of your feet, or is the weight evenly spread between the balls and the heel? We all have different places in the body where tension accumulates.

Our body is where we live and have our being, and meditation is first the practice of coming home to our own body and spending some time there. "I have so many thoughts" or "I'm thinking all the time" is the experience of most first-time meditators. This is like noticing the clutter at home. You don't notice the clutter if you are never there. You must come home and spend some time there in order to notice it. What is your reaction to being aware of the clutter? To run out the door? To be reluctant to come back again? These are common reactions. Many people report having difficulty getting themselves to sit in meditation, and in every meditation group there are one or two who come only once and never again. They have come face-to-face with the clutter and did not like what they saw.

THE HEART-SPACE

The third aspect of coming home is coming home to a heart full of love. Our heart is our emotional home. Whether it is full of love or hate, whether it is full of kindness or anger, the heart-space is where we hold people, and from where we act.

Buddha's default emotion was love. What is yours? Look into the preferences tab of your heart and see. You were able to set the default browser on your computer. Can you also choose the default emotion in your heart?

We *live* in our heart-space. Our emotions control the tones of our voices, the looks in our eyes, and the expressions on our faces. What we put in our heart and what we choose to keep there are too important to leave to chance. Our parents are no longer responsible for the contents of our heart—*we* are. Evolution and culture did put "cookies" there, just as many websites put them on our computers, but we can disable those cookies on our computers, and we can also disable them in our hearts with mindfulness if we do not like what they are doing to us. We do that by scanning our thoughts. If we find negative thoughts in our hearts, we can delete them. If loving thoughts do not come automatically, we can do a search for them, and download them to the desktop of our heart-space.

The home is where the heart is, but when you are always somewhere else, your heart can get all mixed up. Come back home and stay around for a while. Lovingly take care of your home. Put some flowers on the table. Water them regularly. Enjoy the moment, enjoy being home. As you take care and put order in your heart, you will feel more comfortable staying in the moment. Cultivate flowers of peace, berries of love, herbs of wisdom there, and make it into a lovely garden.

This practice is available to all of us. But beware: being in the moment can be pretty abstract-sounding if we do not ground it in the breath. Come back to your breath, and you will also be coming back to the present moment. As we practice coming back to and staying in the body, we get in the habit of seeing it as our home. As we do that, we are more motivated to take good care of our bodies, to eat well, to exercise, and to spend more time outdoors. It is surprising how people often take better care of their house than of their body. You can always get a new house, but you cannot get a new body. People who would not make an open fire on the living room floor nevertheless are smokers.

Our feelings and emotions influence our thoughts, our speech, and the way we listen.

As our heart-space becomes a more beautiful place, we feel more at ease and comfortable there. However, be forewarned: it takes some time to grow a garden, lovingly plant seeds, water the flowers, and weed. It also takes some patience. A garden is never finished. It needs constant attention and moment-to-moment awareness.

PRACTICE SONG
"Coming Back Home"

As you breathe, let your breath bring you back to your home within,
As you walk, let your steps bring you back to your home within.
As you listen, let the sound bring you back to your home within,
As you look, let the light bring you back to your home within.
Come back to your home within, with each breath
Come back to your home within, with each step
As you breathe, let your breath bring you back to your home within,
As you walk, let your steps bring you back to your home within.

You can breathe or walk in two ways: while listening to the physical sensations coming from your body, or while thinking of other things. The first way keeps you here and in the moment. If you have temporarily become lost in thought, it brings you back "home." The second way takes you away from the here-and-now. It takes you to a different time and place somewhere out in mind-space.

As you practice with this song, let each breath bring you home, in all three senses of the word. When you walk, let the mind do the walking as well as the body. Don't let the mind get ahead of the body and go to your destination alone. Let it walk hand in hand with the body. When you eat, let the mind eat as well. When you lie down to sleep, let the mind also lie down. Let the body and mind lie on the bed hand in hand and go to sleep together.

Don't let sounds take you away from your home in the here-and-now. The bird is not out there—it is in your head. It is singing its song intimately in your ear. That is how birdsongs and the mindfulness bell bring us to the moment. That is also how the bird can come and nestle in our heart-space.

Even thoughts can bring us to the here-and-now if we go beyond them. The image of your boyfriend or girlfriend is in your head here and now, but it is only an image, not an actual person. If the actual person were in your head, you would need a very large head, and a very strong neck! The actual person may be somewhere else, but her image is *here*.

We own the images we make about other people, about our partners and children. We own these images, because we are the ones who make them—they are ours in a very real way. Indeed, if we were artists and had the talent to turn our mental images into portraits, we would have proprietary rights to them. We could copyright them and sell them. But we do not own the people represented by our mental images. This creates confusion for some people—the image looks very much like the person, and we confuse the two. As a result, we may assume that the real person is somehow like the image in our heads. But the real person is always ready to surprise us—there is more to them than we realize. The real person is also always ready to show that, unlike the image in our heads, they do not belong to us.

14

A RELATIONSHIP IS EVERY STEP

Thich Nhat Hanh famously said, "Peace is every step." In saying it, he did not mean to imply a lack of commitment. He meant that peace is, above all, a journey. A relationship is also a journey.

In a *New York Times* article, Mary Elizabeth Williams quotes the words of the man she shares her life with: "I used to think the relationship part of my life was settled and I never had to worry about it. Now I think, if you love someone, you have to take it one day at a time. And you have to work at it one day at a time." She loves what she hears and mentally commits to her relationship once more as she listens to him. Here again, there is no lack of commitment—she relates that her partner stuck with her through her grueling ordeal with malignant melanoma, day by day.

"But he and I have learned, because we have had to, the difference between the illusion of security and the liberating joy of the present, between obligation and choice," continues Williams. "And choice, terrifying as it can be, is so much better. We had to leave each other to discover that: to understand what it really means to decide to be with a person, one day at a time, however many days there may be. Love isn't a fortress. It isn't a locked room." The man she is writing about, her present relationship partner, is also her ex-husband.

In the end, it is not marriage that keeps a couple together, it is the other way around—the couple decide each day to keep their relationship going, and that is why they stay married. "Marriage is the leading cause of divorce," said Groucho Marx. I take Groucho to mean that marriage is a package that may include unexpressed expectations. It may mean a feeling of entrapment. It may mean that all the choices of a lifetime were made once and for all, and there are no choices left anymore, only obligations. It may mean that marriage was seen only as an end, and not as a journey.

Thich Nhat Hanh considers that there are four indispensable elements in a loving relationship. I will describe these in my own words:

FRIENDSHIP

The basic human bond of friendship ties a couple together above and beyond romantic attachment. We understand our friends, we know them well. Or perhaps it is the other way around, and we become friends with people we understand. One way or another, we are kind to our friends, we do things for them to make them happy.

CARE AND CONCERN

We care for our relationship partner—if they are going through a rough patch, we try to be there for them. We are concerned about their well-being, and we show our concern by helping when the opportunity presents itself. We try to cheer them up if they are feeling sad.

FUN

We have fun together. We celebrate our good times together. We take pleasure in each other's accomplishments and success.

SELF-REGULATION AND EQUANIMITY

Self-regulation is essential for a good relationship, for until we develop some self-regulation skills, our relationships tend to be chaotic.

MORE ABOUT SELF-REGULATION

Self-regulation is a dynamic concept; it is not something we can achieve once and for all. In life, we are always losing and regaining our balance—we cannot even walk without losing our balance. When we walk, we first move the body forward a little, so it gets a little out of balance. But we do not panic—we calmly take a step forward to regain our balance. Running is even more dynamic—if you cannot regain your balance by taking a step as when your foot encounters a rock, the root of a tree, or another object on the ground, you stumble and fall down.

Self-regulation refers to the ability to find one's equilibrium over and over again as circumstances and our own needs push us out of balance. In this sense, it is akin to resilience.

Toddlers and young children fall down more often—their physical self-regulation skills are not yet fully developed. They also cry more often than adults. Their emotional self-regulation skills are also not mature yet.

Composure, levelheadedness, and stability are some of the meanings of equanimity. With equanimity, there is less drama in a relationship, and meditation fosters equanimity.

CONNECT IN ORDER TO STAY IN THE PRESENT

You have to build some kind of a life in the present in order to stay in the present. If you do not have a life now, it is easier to slip into the habit of living in the past—even though it is not real, it may be more interesting than what you now have. Sometimes elderly people who have lost spouses, are not working anymore, and have also lost many of their friends get into the habit of mentally living in the past. They have gotten into that state by neglecting the present and mentally living in the past, and their restricted lifestyle now keeps them mired in the past, because it seems more interesting than the empty present.

Nor is this exclusively a state of mind of the elderly. I have seen it in some middle-aged people who have suffered a loss and are unwilling to move forward because of their fears. However, life does not stop—it moves on without them and leaves them behind. To live in the present moment, we need to engage with the present moment, and a relationship is a good way to do that—connection is the essence of life.

JOINT SELF-REGULATION

Ballet dancers and figure skaters develop a special relationship with their partners. They trust their partners so that they can allow themselves to get out of balance, knowing that their partner will not let them fall down. A good relationship can be like a couples dance in ballet, where self-regulating capacity is shared. The life of a couple is dynamic like a dance—it is not static like marble statues in a museum.

Joint self-regulation is also taking care of the mental state of your partner. A smile and a word of appreciation is a way of doing that. Just as positive self-talk may help you to keep your own mental state high, positive conversation can do the same for your partner.

Here is a poem that connects *relationship* to the feeling of *home* discussed in the previous chapter:

"THE HOME OF THE HEART"

Ducks are diving for weeds near the rocky shore.
As I watch them, I notice:

a cozy intimacy radiates from the female and the male in the center
as they move together on the unmarked waters
dining on tasty morsels
and turning toward each other
again and again—they are a couple.

Home is also this centeredness on each other
I muse
even on moving waters,
and the willingness to ignore
the vast spaces around.
The homeless
have given this up, or have never found it. (J. E.)

COEXIST

The *COEXIST* sign, which is popping up in more and more places these days, captures another aspect of a good relationship. In some versions, this sign plays with the shape of the letters so that it expresses its meaning graphically—the *T* looks like a Christian cross, the *X* like a Jewish star, and the symbols for male and female decorate the letter *E*. For, fulfilling and "romantic" as it can be, a close relationship is also a test of our ability to share a living space. Only three syllables separate "close" from "claustrophobic." For me, *COEXIST* sums up in a light vein other significant qualities such as respect, tolerance, and the ability to give a person some leg room. An important challenge of a relationship is the need to be good roommates as well as intimate partners, and a measure of equanimity is essential for harmonious coexisting. Equanimity calms down feelings that may otherwise be going up and down like a yo-yo. Meditation gives us perspective—we can hear our own brain messages of criticism as well as infatuation with some detachment—they have to do as much with us as with the other. The other person is a mirror as well as a window.

CONNECTION WITHOUT OWNERSHIP

If your love is only a will to possess, it's not love.
—THICH NHAT HANH

Without a partner or children, we can feel alone in the world and suffer from loneliness. But if we have a partner and children, some of us assume a stance of ownership toward them and suffer from the resulting conflicts. An attitude of ownership comes out in controlling behaviors and results in frustration, because other people are not keen to be owned. My child is not mine alone. Apart from obviously belonging to the other parent in equal measure, she also belongs to herself, and to her relatives and friends. These people also describe my child as "mine"—*my friend, my cousin,* or *my granddaughter.* I may think that belonging to me trumps all these other claims, but there is a basis for conflict there—the others may not agree with me.

In another, deeper sense, a child is a child of the Earth, like a flower is a child of the Earth—no flower claims another flower as "mine." Your child is a child of nature. The air she breathes sustains her as much as mother's milk. Gravity holds her as much as your arms do. And her evolutionary heritage affects her more than the color of her eyes that she inherited from you.

Your child is also a child of her culture and time. Her behavior is shaped by what she sees on the TV screen and what she reads in magazines or on the Internet. She might even regard you as a relic of a time long gone and not identify with your views.

There is more. Even the mother's milk you give your baby is not entirely yours. Your conscious mind, the mind that comes up with feelings of ownership, has no clue about how to produce mother's milk. It is nature that does it through you. It is also nature that created your child through you. You would not know where to begin producing a human being otherwise—the formula has not yet been discovered and posted on the Internet. When we label nature's child as "mine," we miss the sacred dimension of parenthood.

Similarly, what you call "my body" was created by nature and evolution according to conditions on Earth. You do not really own it. It has a mind of its own and gets sick without your permission. It will even decide to die someday without asking you. Without a measure of equanimity, this perceived lack of control creates stress.

TRUE BELONGINGS

It is best to reserve feelings of ownership toward your actions. "My actions are my true belongings," says Thich Nhat Hanh. My actions, and not my possessions, are my real belongings. My behavior is truly mine, and not my house, my car, or any people toward whom I may feel possessive. Our actions are often longer lasting than we are—they echo on and on like ripples on a calm lake. That conviction must have played a part in motivating Buddha to leave his princely estate and take up the homeless life to teach the Dharma. History has proved him right. There is no trace left of his princely estate now, but his true belongings—his actions—are still echoing through the world. If you are looking for proof of the truth of that saying, you need go no further.

But it is not only larger-than-life actions such as those of the Buddha that go on and on. A steady dose of kindness and mother's milk enables a bear cub to survive and become an adult. That bear may end up being the progenitor of a thousand generations of bears through many centuries. In our human world, acts of kindness and connection often go further in creating happiness than big investment portfolios and palatial homes.

OPENING THE HEART

Our ability to be in the body nourishes our capacity to connect with the reality of another person instead of with a *concept* of the other person.

Expectations are part of our concept of the other person—of putting the other in a box of our own making.

Idealizing the other person is another way of relating to a concept rather than the reality of another.

The more we are open to our own reality, the more we can appreciate the reality of another. With mindfulness meditation, a relationship can be a tool for growth, and growth a tool for better relationships.

The heart opens through understanding.

The heart opens through love.

I have found the most beautiful description of love in Thich Nhat Hanh's book *Teachings on Love*:

Through my love for you, I want to express my love for the whole cosmos, the whole of humanity, and all beings. By living with you, I want to learn to love everyone and all species. If I succeed in loving you, I will be able to love everyone and all species on Earth. [. . .] This is the real message of love.

TREASURING YOUR LOVE

A treasure is in the eye of the beholder.

Here is a parable from *Aesop's Fables*:

A cock, scratching the ground for something to eat, turned up a jewel that had by chance been dropped there. "Ho!" said he, "a fine thing you are, no doubt, and, had your owner found you, great would his joy have been. But for me, give me a single grain of corn before all the jewels in the world."

It takes two to create a treasure: the treasure and the treasurer. Love transforms a person or an object into a treasure. Gold by itself would be no treasure, just a shiny yellow metal. It is our love for it that gives gold its value and elevates it to the status of treasure. Ditto for a man or a woman. We become a treasure in the eyes of someone who loves us, and something wonderful happens to us when we are so treasured—we begin to appreciate ourselves more.

The Taj Mahal was built by Shah Jahan for the love of his life, Mumtaz Mahal. Her name means "Jewel of the Palace." During their life together, Mumtaz Mahal gave birth to fourteen children. After her death, Shah Jahan spent twenty-two years building the monument to his love. If she had not met Shah Jahan and, more important, if he had not cherished her inner and outer beauty, would she still be a jewel? Love not only transforms the loved one—the "treasure"—it also changes the one who recognizes the treasure. It transforms both the lover and the beloved.

This is also true of the "ordinary" Buddhist bow of greeting if done consciously. When we bow to someone, we are bowing to the seeds of mindfulness, beauty, and awakening that are present in that person. The one who bows also cherishes those qualities in herself, and the act of bowing renews the consciousness of her own positive qualities.

PRACTICE SONG
"The Light in Each One Shines and Shines"

The light in each one shines and shines,
That's what makes the world bright.
It makes the stars bright in the night,
It makes the flowers a delight.

I've always enjoyed the gospel children's song "This Little Light of Mine." That song has a way of "going over the top" as children's songs sometimes do. Yet I feel that there is a meditation theme in there somewhere, which I tried to bring out in this mantra.

The freshness and inspiration I feel after being in nature comes from absorbing some of the light emanating from the natural world. There are no assumed identities, no cultural distortions in nature. The more we are in touch with our own inner light, the more we appreciate the light emanating from the natural world.

In my kitchen hangs a saying by the Zen master Ryokan: "In this one bowl, there is rice from a thousand households." It would be fair to say that "in this one mind, there is light from a thousand lamps," as many an encounter left a ray of light with me. Can we see the light in the eyes of each person? This light comes from the preciousness of life that each creature embodies, protects, and cherishes. In his book *Peace Is Every Breath*, Thich Nhat Hanh writes, "You can be in touch with a lot of happiness during the time you're washing your face, brushing your teeth, combing your hair, shaving, and showering, if you know how to shine the light of awareness onto each thing you do." This light delights not only its owner but also all who come in contact with it, all who witness it.

"He whose face gives no light, shall never become a star," said William Blake.

Fortunately, many of us go around like fireflies in the night. We'll recognize others' light more easily if we are in touch with our own. Feel your light glow with each breath, as embers do when we blow on them. Feel your light illuminating your corner of the world, making it brighter.

15

MAKE YOUR OWN WEATHER

There's a dark and a troubled side of life;
There's a bright and a sunny side, too;
Keep on the sunny side, always on the sunny side,
Keep on the sunny side of life.

—FROM THE SONG "KEEP ON THE SUNNY SIDE"
BY BLENKHORN AND ENTWISLE

There is more than one kind of weather. There is the external one that the weather forecaster reports on, the weather indoors in our homes and workplaces, and the internal weather in our hearts and minds. We have no control over the external weather. In any case, most of us live indoors now—at home, at work, on the bus, or in the car, and in those places we can create our own weather. Although I live in frosty Canada, it never snows in my living room.

But the weather that makes the biggest difference in our lives is the one in our hearts and minds. "Suffering is not enough. Life is both dreadful and wonderful. How can I smile when I am filled with so much sorrow? It is natural—you need to smile to your sorrow because you are more than your sorrow," says Thich Nhat Hanh.

You do not have to stop there. Once you smile, the ice is broken, and spring is already there. You can let the trickle of your smile turn into a river of laughter. According to neuroscientists, taking oneself lightly and being able to laugh at one-self makes us secrete endorphins, our own "endogenous morphines" that make us feel good and incidentally energize our immune cells as a bonus. It is an open secret that you do not need to take external opioids like prescription painkillers or heroin in order to feel good. You can instead get high on your own smile and laughter, as your body produces its own morphine for you, free of charge. After all, opioids make us feel good because we have built-in receptors for them. And we have receptors for opioids because our own bodies also produce them.

The well-documented "runner's high" is produced by our own endorphins. So is the less well-documented "meditator's high." A study by the School of Behavioral Sciences at the James Cook University of North Queensland, Australia, compared experienced runners and trained meditators. Although running and meditation are so different as activities, the researchers found that mood changes after running and meditating were similar. Compared to pretest moods (and those of a control group), both running and meditating elicited a positive mood change. It turns out that meditation stimulates the pituitary gland and the hypothalamus and releases endorphins. It also increases production of serotonin, dopamine, and melatonin, all related to positive moods, happiness, and relaxation.

We can control our internal weather by choosing the activities we participate in—our internal thermostats are adjustable through our actions. What set the thermostat originally? For some of us, it is genetics. For others, it is upbringing. For others, it is culture or gender. Women laugh a lot more than men. But who cares what the thermostat was set to when you brought it home and opened the package? What is important is not the factory setting, but the level that works best for you, and you can set that level with mindfulness practice.

The weather outside is determined by the elements—by the sun, wind, clouds, and air pressure. It is determined by conditions and is due to chance. Without mindfulness, the weather inside is also determined by chance. Our moods and states of mind just happen. With mindfulness, we become aware that we make our own sunshine and clouds. We make our own weather inside. Once we recognize this, weather-making becomes possible.

Many of us know that this can be done with children. We can manipulate the internal weather of children to a great extent by directing their attention toward positive activities or by giving them a treat. We may also be aware of how our elderly parents make their own weather. If we know someone who is anxious or depressed, it is clear to us that their minds are creating those conditions. Yet often we may not suspect that we have the same power over our own moods and mental states and that we also create our own internal sunshine and clouds.

SELF-REGULATE WITH MUSIC

An excellent way of managing our internal weather, or of self-regulating, is with music. That is one of the reasons why there are a number of practice songs in this book. As you listen to music, part of you is singing along—listening to music involves some degree of participation, even when you are not consciously aware of it. If you are listening to dance music, a part of you is dancing. You are rehearsing the feelings and emotions in the music. If you sing along as you listen, this effect is stronger. There is a lot of junk music out there, about as much as junk food. Junk music is composed to appeal to your ears and to your brain, not to your wisdom. Start with the songs that are part of this book—they will give you a good taste of "health music." Health music is as good for your spirit as health foods are good for your body.

THE CHICKEN OR THE EGG?

Which came first?

Why bother with puzzles when you know that you can start with either—you can start with a chicken and make eggs, or start with eggs and make chickens.

Start where you are.

Do not wait to feel good before you go out for a walk or before you exercise. Sometimes you go out for a walk because you feel good, and sometimes you feel good because you go out for a walk. Couch potatoes, take note. Personally, I sometimes get off the couch because I feel energetic, and sometimes I feel energetic because I got off the couch.

OBSTACLE TO MEDITATION

Similarly, sometimes you meditate because you are in the right mood, and sometimes you get in the right mood because you meditate. We may not feel an urgent need to meditate such as we do for eating or drinking, but we nevertheless feel better if we meditate regularly. Meditation is like exercise in this respect.

Consider that some people can even get dehydrated if they wait till they feel thirsty before drinking water.

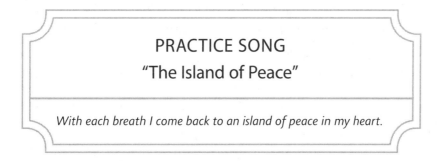

PRACTICE SONG
"The Island of Peace"

With each breath I come back to an island of peace in my heart.

You can sing along with this song while doing walking meditation or before you do sitting meditation. In each case, it will make your practice more meaningful. Let each breath be like a pull on the oars that bring you to the island of peace. Row rhythmically, and with long strokes on a calm lake, and arrive at the island in your heart with each stroke.

As you paint a mental picture of an island of peace, keep in mind that this island is in you. When we visualize an island of peace, we might put ourselves in the picture. In this meditation, it is the other way around—we put the picture inside us. It is the island of peace that is inside us, and we return there with each breath.

If there is no peace in your heart, you will not feel peaceful even when you are physically in a peaceful place. This song will help you develop a peaceful heart so that you can find peace wherever you are.

In the island-of-peace metaphor, the peace in my heart is protected by the expanse of water around the island. I do not have to deny or ignore disturbances. I can see them on the other shore, so to speak, but I'm safe in my refuge. I do not let the disturbances, mental or emotional, invade my mental space, my island. I do not let them get to me. Quite the contrary.

"Try to be a rainbow in someone's cloud," the poet Maya Angelou urged.

16

MEDITATING ON THE BATTLEFIELD

*The wheel turns because
we keep running.*

—ANN BURNETT

The purpose of this chapter is not to win battles but to transform what feels like a battlefield into a garden of peace. It comes near the end of this book, because a battlefield is not the best place to *learn* meditation techniques. It is better to develop meditation skills with formal meditation practice before one can use them in difficult situations. However, this remains an ideal, as people are not always keen to put the energy into it when things are going well for them.

The great classic of Indian spirituality, the Bhagavad Gita, was composed on the battlefield, just before a battle in which almost every man of fighting age was killed. If the prospect of such a battle does not stimulate deep meditation on life and death, what will? What makes battlefield meditation special is the fact that the issues are not theoretical. They are in your face. The meditation training that is practiced in retreats and practice communities is a preparation for contextual meditation, not a substitute for it. Here is one of my favorite verses from the Gita:

"When a person responds to the joys and sorrows of others as if they were his own, he has attained the highest state of spiritual union."

We learn who we are as we watch ourselves in action. As we act, we not only reveal the parts of ourselves that we think we know, but we also discover parts that we do not yet know. Meditation and action are not opposites but complement each other. Meditation is not to be practiced only in meditation rooms with the door closed to the life outside. Meditation needs to be a part of life, part of the revelation of each new moment, each new adventure. Thich Nhat Hanh's wisdom was forged in the heat of the Vietnam War, and the Dalai Lama's peace and compassion withstood the challenge of the Chinese invasion of Tibet. Who knows if these two teachers would have experienced the full flowering of their genius without the test of fire? The test of fire was not a mere distraction. It contributed to their wisdom.

Jesus also lived in turbulent times, against the backdrop of the Roman occupation of Palestine, and died a violent death. Can his teaching and wisdom be separated from his life?

Here is another line of timeless wisdom that comes from another sort of a battlefield—the Nazi concentration camps at Auschwitz:

Everything can be taken from a man but one thing: the last of the human freedoms—to choose one's attitude in any given set of circumstances, to choose one's own way.

—VIKTOR E. FRANKL, *MAN'S SEARCH FOR MEANING*

What makes this sentence outstanding is the extremely difficult circumstances in which it was uttered. Would Frankl have discovered the truth of his message if he himself had not been pushed to the limit, and did not have a personal experience confirming it? What I take home from it is that if Frankl could hold on to a positive attitude in a death camp, I also could do it in the circumstances of my own life that are blissfully much less trying.

BRAINFUL OR MINDFUL?

Identify areas of your life where there is a battle. When a situation arises where you are conflicted, sit for a period of meditation. This is a technique to let the whole of you decide the course of your life, instead of only a part of you. In the presence of a strong emotion such as fear or anger, the voice of the emotion drowns out other voices such as the voice of your values and goals. A period of meditation allows these other voices to be heard. It brings perspective and wisdom to a situation. It brings peace to a battlefield.

TAKING A MEDITATION BREAK

I sometimes feel a kind of "meditation hunger." It usually comes from a lack of mental clarity or a feeling of having lost my way—not in a big existential kind of way like on the highway of life, but more like in the woods while taking a walk. It is more a feeling of indecision than of being truly lost. A short period of meditation later, I feel invigorated, full of enthusiasm, and I have a clear idea as to which way I want to go. Sometimes, it is in a totally different direction from what I imagined before sitting down. Meditation has opened doors that I did not even know were there. It feels like consulting the larger part of who I am—it is like connecting with the source.

Einstein's well-known words come to mind again—*We can't solve problems by using the same kind of thinking we used when we created them.* When I try to solve the little problems of everyday life consciously, I may notice that my mind is running around the ruts that created the problem in the first place. A period of meditation stops the running around and gives the ruts a break. Only then is it possible to start fresh in a new direction. For me, this is a recipe for inspired living.

WHERE IS THE BATTLEFIELD?

For some of us, the battlefield can be where we do our daily battles with what to eat and how much to eat.

Meditate there. Sit for a few minutes before eating. Breathe in and out, and put everything out of your mind for a while. Then get in touch with the one who is eating. Who is filling up the plate? Is it only the taste buds? Is there a person behind those taste buds? Which is bigger, the person or the taste buds?

Feel the taste buds. Listen to their message, then talk back to them and calm them down. Are they bullies? Are they used to getting their way? Explain the facts of life to them calmly. Who is in charge? Yes, the taste buds want tasty stuff, and lots of it. That is their mission in life, their job. Congratulate them for doing their job with such enthusiasm. Then get in touch and stay in touch with the rest of you that may have other missions, other goals. If the stomach wants to be full and blissfully bulging, offer it a glass of lemon water or a cup of herbal tea. Mentally recite your values about a healthy life. This is not that different from talking to a child who wants this, that, and the other. Children also see only a part and not the whole. Meditate until you are at peace and feel whole.

A GODDESS OF PEACE

Irene (pronounced Ear-in-eh) is the goddess of peace in Greek mythology. In art she is shown as an attractive woman holding a cornucopia (a symbol of plenty represented by a horn full of flowers) in her right hand. Unfortunately, she is not always present in our workplaces or homes. The first step in bringing Irene to these places is to give her a place in our hearts. We can do that with a period of peace meditation.

MEDITATION THEME
Peace Meditation

Breathe in peace, breathe out peace.

Become aware that a part of you wants to do, do, do,

    and a part of you wants to relax and de-stress.

Both parts are you. You do not want a battle between them.

You want peace between them.

Find your inner smile and contentment as you breathe,

    dwell in peaceful concentration on the breath.

Feel your face muscles relax.

Feel the extra tension drain away from your body.

Visualize yourself holding a cup of plenty in your hands,

    and radiating peace: There is enough everywhere,

    enough food in the cupboard, enough clothes,

    and enough time. Smile.

Visualize yourself doing things from a place of relaxation.

With peace in your heart.

Visualize doing things from a place of plenty

    instead of from a place of scarcity.

Make peace between the doer inside you, and the one who

    wants to relax.

You can do things and relax at the same time.

Pick something that needs to be done,

    and visualize yourself doing it in a relaxed way

    without hurry, without stress, and with a smile.

Does the mere thought of doing something bring tension to

    parts of your body?

Could this be habit energy?

Visualize yourself going through an everyday activity like get-

    ting dressed

    or walking to your car.

Go through it a few times in your mind until you can mentally

    do it without tension, and with a smile.

THE CHALLENGE OF CONCENTRATION

Concentration is a big challenge, especially when a wound is fresh in the mind—when we are faced with a mental problem or when we are severely stressed.

Francis was one of my meditation coaching clients. He had been severely depressed for thirty years, and doctors and psychotherapists had given up on him. He was referred for mindfulness meditation coaching. But he could not concentrate enough to do guided meditation. I knew that he enjoyed music, so I started introducing him to mindfulness songs. We would sing a song together several times, then talk about its meaning and how to use it in everyday life. Then I would ask him to hum or sing it as often as he could during the week.

Melodies stick in the mind without effort. The words that accompany the melodies come along for the ride. The result mimics concentration. One only has to "activate" the song, and it will take over the mind, providing an antidote to invasive negative feelings.

You can practice like Francis. Listen to a practice song several times until it sticks in your mind and on your lips. Then let it repeat mentally during the day.

17

MOVING ON

> *In each of us, there is a young, suffering child. We have all had times of difficulty as children and many of us have experienced trauma.*
> —THICH NHAT HANH

A human baby is born half-baked and needs much care for a long time to come. She has no language skills and cannot say what she wants or what is bothering her. This creates a minefield for misunderstandings and unintentional hurt. In addition, a child's needs are not the only needs in the household—other siblings and parents have their own needs, and sometimes these other needs are more urgent and trump the child's needs. At times there are also emotional storms in a household. This creates additional chances for unintended neglect or emotional wounds.

We all have scars from the time of childhood. Our challenge is to move on—

to understand that this is part of our human heritage, to have compassion for ourselves and for our kindhearted caregivers, take time to heal our scars with understanding, but then move on with our lives.

Taking care of a baby is a challenge. I remember a time when my daughter was doing her first stint as a babysitter. I think this may have been the baby's first stint with a babysitter as well—a tricky combination. We got a call. The baby would not stop crying and go to sleep.

I asked if the baby was wearing a sweater. Yes, she was. It was a warm summer night, and I asked my daughter to take off the sweater and see what happened.

A few minutes later she called to say that the baby had stopped crying and was asleep. This story makes me look good, but when my daughter was a baby herself, we could not always figure out why she was crying. We just tried one thing after another and kept our fingers crossed.

We have all had times of difficulty as children. Thich Nhat Hanh's words are no exaggeration. Under the best of circumstances, the baby's helplessness and undeveloped brain creates problems not only for her caregivers but also for the baby herself. Unlike a baby deer, a human baby cannot survive without compassion, but our compassion is all mixed up with our beliefs and social customs. We are still trying to figure out whether circumcision is a manifestation of our compassion or whether it is child abuse, and whether moms should be tigers or pussycats.

From this springs a host of developmental challenges.

The supply of compassion is also limited—until recently, many women of childbearing age were always either pregnant or recovering from giving birth. They had to balance the "crying" needs of more than one offspring. Of course, that was not all. The mother had her own needs—she might have been kept awake at night and might have needed some rest or extra sleep. She might also have been already pregnant with another child and low on energy.

"Human beings respond to shock and developmental/relational trauma by disassociating and disconnecting. The result is a dimming down of the life force that leaves a person, to varying degrees, exiled from life," write Laurence Heller and Aline LaPierre in *Healing Developmental Trauma*. They also write that we have all experienced developmental trauma to some degree, a statement that echoes Thich Nhat Hanh's words.

A baby's helplessness creates a big challenge, for the mother as well as for the baby. A mother deer continues to go about her business of feeding, resting, moving about, or even migrating nonchalantly as her offspring take care of themselves and follow in close contact. A human mother needs to change her lifestyle drastically in order to devote much attention to her helpless babies. For one reason or another, she may not always do that successfully. Perhaps she does not have enough money. Perhaps she has a difficult partner or no partner. Perhaps she has her own problems. All of this contributes to Thich Nhat Hanh's statement that *We have all had times of difficulty as children*. He is describing a fact of life. Having times of difficulty as children is not an exception to the rule. It is the rule. Many of us have experienced difficulties later on in life as well.

MOVING ON

In one retreat, a woman asked Thich Nhat Hanh if he could suggest anything for stopping her recurring nightmares. To my surprise, Thich Nhat Hanh replied that he also has nightmares sometimes and said a few words to describe his wartime experiences in Vietnam. My mind went back to a passage I had read in one of his books where he describes a napalm bomb exploding in the next room where a friend of his was sleeping. Another passage describes coming home one day to find his roommates shot and lying in pools of blood.

He has moved on, although he has more than his share of scars.

"All healing is inevitably heart-centered," writes Dr. Marcey Shapiro in her book *Freedom from Anxiety*. Our wounds are emotional, they are in the heart, and that is where they must be encountered and healed so we *can* move on.

CHANGING THE PAST

Thich Nhat Hanh has worked to change the past, not by dwelling on the past, but by moving on. He contributed to stopping the Vietnam War by touring the United States, giving lectures, and leading peace marches. He has been speaking out against war and promoting peace ever since—a few years ago he even held a retreat for members of the U.S. Congress.

Thich Nhat Hanh has not forgotten the past, but instead of crippling him, his memories energize him—they keep motivating him to work tirelessly to promote peace within and peace in the world. Knowing the details of his life makes us realize that there are also personal reasons why he has made it his life's work to spread the teachings on mindfulness.

GETTING STUCK IN THE PAST

In my work teaching mindfulness to individuals and groups, I have met more than one person whose psychotherapy merely served the purpose of getting them mired in the past. Nadia, an attractive sixty-six-year-old blonde, told me that she has been in therapy constantly since she was fifteen. Over several sessions, I have had much difficulty getting her to talk about the present instead of the past. It had become a habit. Sample talk: "I smoke because my parents locked me up in a closet when I was young." She alternates between periods of parent-bashing and self-bashing (shame) and has no energy left for the present moment. Jason, a handsome thirty-nine-year-old man, has been in psychotherapy for anxiety for six years. He still experiences the same anxiety as before but is addicted to going to see his therapist every week to talk about his past. He is convinced that there is something deeply wrong with him, and soon he will find out what it is, and then everything will be resolved.

SELF-REGULATE NOW

Those who medicate and those who meditate have one thing in common: they are trying to self-regulate in the present moment. If trauma and past wounds stayed in the past, there would not be a problem—you could go on from there. Walking in the woods, I sometimes see a tree that has encountered a rock as a sapling and grew around it. It did not have much of a choice—it was either grow that way or not grow at all. That was the condition. It accepted the condition, accepted life, and took its chances. Now it has become a big tree, even a huge tree, but it still has a twisted trunk. The kink has stayed in the history of the tree. It is still there, but the leaves in the upper branches are living in the present, basking in the sun, and waving to me in the wind. They are not bothered by past memories.

But we are not like the tree. Our past and our present are inextricably mixed up in our living memory—for we not only have a historical memory, we also have a living memory. The past masquerades as the present for us when we remember it in our thoughts—we relive the past as the present over and over again. The tree self-regulated once, dealt with the condition it encountered growing up, and did not look back. We look back, and we have to self-regulate over and over again as we look back.

The power of now is that it emulates the tree. With mindfulness practice, we live in the moment, experiencing the joys and the sadness of this moment, instead of the joys and the sadness of another moment in the past. Like the sapling, we may have encountered a problem growing up. Those were the conditions of our life at the time—we had to grow in those conditions. Mindfulness practice says, "Open your eyes and see the sun." Open your eyes to this moment. The memory pulls us back to the past. Mindfulness practice pulls us up to the present.

TURN THE PAGE

It does not have to be trauma. Even when reading a book, I sometimes notice myself still mulling over what I read on the previous page. My brain has this propensity. Mindfulness practice fulfills a need for me—a need for continual refreshment, a need to experience the freshness of each moment. This is also part of what I mean by going from "brainfulness" toward mindfulness. Without mindfulness, I would be a prisoner of that tendency of my brain.

Whatever has happened in the past, we still have to deal with present issues in the present moment. We have to self-regulate in the present. Mindfulness meditation keeps us focused on the present and, as we keep staying in the present, the past slowly loses its power to bind us.

PRACTICE SONG
"Lay Down Your Burden"

Lay down your burden; lay down your load,
Give your shoulders a rest, give your heart back its wings.
Then pick it up again, pick it up with love,
And carry it with joy, it's lighter that way.

The seeds of this song were sown at a retreat where I was offering private consultations to the retreatants. A retired university professor came to see me. He was very anxious about the environment to the point of having recurring nightmares. "What kind of a world am I leaving my grandchildren?" was a disturbing thought constantly on his mind.

I told him that I shared his concern about the environment. But I wanted to go further—I wanted to ease his distress without trying to "meditate" him out of it with my words. One can think about our long-suffering planet in two ways: with love and compassion, or with fear and anxiety. Fear and anxiety tend to paralyze us. They crowd our mind with negative thoughts. In contrast, love and compas-

JOSEPH EMET • 201

sion are positive emotions. They bring with them positive energies that can heal us and move us forward.

I asked him to concentrate on his love for his grandchildren, and to gradually expand that feeling of love to encompass all beings. "Let your love tell you what to do, not your fear and anxiety," was my message. I wanted him to spend the rest of the retreat immersed in love and compassion rather than mired in negativity.

I hope this encounter sowed some beneficial seeds in this man. It did in me: I left that meeting repeating the phrase *Lay down your burden* to myself, aware that anxious thoughts had become a burden to him. For me, mentally repeating a phrase is often the first step in writing a song. One day, the rest of the song popped in my head as I was getting into my car.

What burdens are you carrying now? Are they getting you down? Can you replace your sense of obligation with love?

18

AN INSPIRED LIFE

If you think you are too small to make a difference, try sleeping with a mosquito.

—THE DALAI LAMA

The first step in making a difference in the world is self-regulation and living in the light of our own values. We cannot offer something to the world that we do not ourselves have. As we achieve equanimity with meditation, we suffer less, and we inflict less suffering on the people in our lives. We are less likely to confuse our own needs with the needs of other people. And we are more likely to see where our particular mix of talent and inclination can be helpful.

We can learn to self-regulate with meditation instead of with medication, alcohol, cigarettes, and food. Meditation in schools, hospitals, clinics, and prisons can be useful for many people. As we recognize the biases of our brains toward more power, more possessions, more this and more that, we are less influenced by them and are more able to follow our values and live simply and with more wisdom.

Ultimately, "brainfulness" may be incompatible with a sustainable lifestyle. It is predominately the male brain that is programmed to spend so much of its energy to conquer, to dominate, and to fight to assert itself. A huge proportion of the Earth's resources are spent supporting the programming of our brain. According to UNICEF, we could meet basic human needs for everyone if just ten percent of the world's military spending were redirected toward that purpose.

It has been said that we are not rational animals but rationalizing animals. We will find a way to justify our aggressiveness in some way—as God's command, as patriotism, or as economic interest. It is not rare to find on the same page of a daily newspaper a report moaning that we have spent less money buying things in the last quarter and another report lamenting the accelerating warming of the climate. Do we notice the connection here and the irony of this double lament?

As documented in this book, "brainfulness" is not compatible with our personal happiness either. The brain keeps repeating messages of stress, depression, or anxiety if we have a challenge with those issues. If we have no such challenges, the brain pulls us back to the past or forward to the future with its thinking, daydreams, or ruminations and keeps us from enjoying the present.

GENDER ISSUES

"By all standards, men are on average twenty times more aggressive than women, something that a quick look around the prison system will confirm," writes Dr. Louann Brizendine in her book *The Female Brain*. The male propensity for abstract thinking is another inclination we have. We are seduced by ideologies such as communism and Marxism, and even our compassion can be ideological. In order to bring our compassion down to earth, we need to find a balance between body and mind. Women's compassion is often more embodied and elemental. We all owe our existence on Earth to a mother's care and kindness. However, stereotyping can create its own distortions, as we all reflect our gender in individual ways.

WHO ARE WE?

The ancient Greeks viewed us as chameleons. At that time, a woman might go to the temple of Aphrodite, the seductive and sexy goddess of love; to the temple of Athena, the industrious goddess of crafts and civilization; to the temple of Artemis, the wild woman who wandered about naked in the woods and hunted; or to the temple of Hera, the domesticated housewife. She might go to more than one temple. As the Greeks saw it, all women did not have the same nature. Venus, or Aphrodite as the Greeks called her, was only one of her guises.

Indeed, as I look at how modern women are, from glamour girl to soldier to judge to member of the Olympic hockey team, it seems presumptuous to try to reduce them to "Venusians" or to any other stereotype. Ditto for men.

Yet gender differences exist, and meditating on them has brought me much insight, and you may also find it enlightening, or at least entertaining. Insight does not have to be put into words, and it has the virtue of being about the here-and-now, whereas generalizations pretend to apply to all people.

PRACTICE SONG
"Be Yourself"

Like the oak tree in the woods,
Like the daisy on the path,
Like the swallow dancing in the air,
Be yourself, be yourself,
Like the sun that warms us all, be yourself, your true self.
Let the traffic speed away,
Let the others have their say,
Let the children be themselves and play,

Be yourself, be yourself,
Like the Earth that holds us all, be yourself, your true self.
Mind your spirit all day long,
Let your talk be like a song,
Let your walk be like a dance,
Be yourself, be yourself,
Like the moon that lights up the sky, be yourself, your true self.

As this song reminds us, it is the same energy of the sun, the moon, and the Earth that is the source of our consciousness and our love. This energy animates us. Fears and anxieties, on the other hand, dampen our animation and darken our flame. Can we stay focused on what makes us go, rather than on what holds us back, on the light of our flame instead of on the darkness that surrounds the flame?

It is easier to be peaceful and calm in a Zendo or in a forest. In those places, we are sucking in the calm that pervades the surroundings. We open ourselves up to this calm and peaceful atmosphere. But there is a downside to being open this way and always expecting peace and calm to come to us from the outside. For what are we to do when there is no peace and calm in our surroundings—in the middle of traffic, in a big city, or in a situation of conflict?

We have to find peace and quiet inside.

In these situations, mindfulness can act like a sort of second skin, shielding and protecting us from the toxic effects of the environment. There is no reason why peace and calm should always come from the outside in. The arrow can also go in the other direction—from the inside out. We first need to develop the protective skin of mindfulness and cultivate an oasis of peace and calm in our heart.

Mood contagion is the ability of someone's anger or sadness to affect us and even overwhelm us, or the ability of a giggle to spread around the room. But mood contagion does not always have to come from the outside in. Picture yourself in the presence of the Buddha. His calm and peace are powerful, even in his pictures and statues—that is why an image of the Buddha often decorates a meditation space. As we get in touch with and develop our mindfulness, we also touch the same power. We *become* the Zendo and the forest.

TEACHING BY PRESENCE

Mood contagion was an important issue for Sheila, a psychologist in her fifties. She told me that she no longer had the patience to listen to her clients. She found it draining to listen to their complaints. This is also an important issue for many parents who have to listen to siblings quibble about everything. If our inner serenity is not strong enough, we get caught up in others' complaints and dissatisfactions, and we allow our spirit to get contaminated by their conflicts.

The alternative is to develop our inner peace through meditation. As we practice smiling to our own negative bias without taking it seriously, we develop the ability to listen to others' complaints in the same way. We can let others "catch" our serenity instead of catching their dissatisfaction.

Our ability to be ourselves does not require anyone else's permission or even cooperation. It does not require others to stop being who they are. It requires only our ability to be in touch with who *we* are and our willingness to let that "little light" of ours to shine forth.

The third verse is a reminder to be constant in our mindfulness practice.

A song is a living thing—it is not discursive discourse. The voice and vocal expression of the singer are part of the song—we can even appreciate a song in a foreign language if we like the singer. A joyful song does not only talk about joy, it also shows it.

Ditto for a dance—a dancer does not only cover the distance when she walks. She also illuminates it.

EXPANDING THE SENSE OF SELF

At the most profound level, we are not whole by ourselves—we are *part* of the whole. There is a Native American tradition of depicting a person with her natural environment—together with the sun, moon, and trees—and the totem animal of her tribe that illustrates this wholeness. As we reach out for a wholeness that is bigger than our individual self, we look for community, we get pets, we buy plants for the house, we cultivate a garden, we have relationships, and we have children. Our plants and our cats are totally self-centered, and we love them—they are being themselves, and that is what we want from them. Our dogs are centered on us, and we also love them—in a different way. Our children are self-centered. Some of us expect that, and some of us have difficulty with it.

And our partners? The right mix continues to baffle us despite reams of books by experts.

Our awareness of who we are expands in circles, noticing and integrating elements of wholeness that are all around us. Can we be complete by ourselves without including our environment? Some years ago Tom Lehrer sang,

If you visit American city
You will find it very pretty
Just two things of which you must beware
Don't drink the water and don't breathe the air.

Things have gotten worse since then, not better. Now, all cities everywhere have environmental challenges. We would not throw garbage on the floor at home—our home is part of our sense of self. But we throw it into our rivers and seas because those are not part of our sense of self. We do not seem to consider the Earth our home. As we achieve a more inclusive sense of self, we become enriched, not impoverished. Including the vast ocean in my sense of self adds to my sense of self. It does not diminish it.

Expanding our sense of self replaces the stone wall around our "property," around who we think we are, with a boundary marker made of a row of flowers. It makes it possible to take ourselves more lightly—we do not need to carry that stone wall around anymore. We also become more inclusive, more willing to include others in our circle of love. And we move toward wholeness and healing in a tangible way.

AFTERWORD: NO REGRETS

Hello darkness, my old friend,
I've come to talk with you again . . .

—**FROM THE SONG "THE SOUND OF**
SILENCE" BY SIMON & GARFUNKEL

I'm writing this on a beautiful spring day in May. The lilacs, Saskatoon berries, and cherry trees in my yard are in bloom. My neighbor's magnolia is all decked out in white and pink, and not a leaf is in sight—all its exuberance is going into flowering, attracting, and reproduction. I watch a blackbird as it lands on a branch, tweets, pecks at an insect, and vibrates its tail with enthusiasm.

Do you have regrets about something you did, or about the way you were in the past? Maybe something you did still bothers you? There's fodder for a lifetime of regretting for all or us if we want to go that way. We were all touchingly innocent, heartbreakingly unwise, and woefully ignorant at some point in our lives. We could not control our bowels, we burped up after we ate, and we were illiterate. We could not even spell our names. Brain scientists say that our brains did not reach full maturity until we were in our twenties. It is natural that we said and did things we would not say or do now. Come back to the present moment as all of nature is doing now—the cold and snowy days of winter are all forgotten, and the ebullience of spring rules the day.

Whether the regretful incident happened yesterday or ten years ago, the brain would like you to go back and do it differently. Do not play its game. Calmly inform your brain that as much as this may be desirable, the laws of physics do not allow it. The remedy for the pain that regret causes is to come back to the breath—to come to the present moment and inhabit it fully. The pain slowly recedes as you do that.

We all learn. We all grow. That is who we are—learners and growers. If you are regretting something, that only means that you are growing. It means that you know better now. It is a cause for celebration, not sorrow. Thank your lucky stars for the opportunity you have had for growth, for acquiring wisdom, and go forward with joy. Do not get stuck mentally rehearsing old mistakes over and over. Identify with the chameleon in you that changes and grows.

You are who you are here and now. Here and now. All else is history.

Is there no value in remembering the past?

Of course there is. It is a wonderful way of developing understanding and compassion.

Compassion for the weak—the weak and the helpless—like we were as babies.

Compassion for those who make mistakes—like the ones we made.

And understanding for those who get stuck in regret. We know how they feel.

We got a high school diploma not because we knew everything when we entered first grade. We got it because we learned and grew during our time in school. The school of life is no different. Stay fresh like the green plant that makes flowers year after year. There is learning after graduation, work after retirement, and life after life: generations of children are waiting in line for their turn to experience life on this planet.

Identify with the life force that makes us flourish and thrive.

Be who you are now, and use your understanding and compassion in some way to help others.

That is the best way to make up for old mistakes.

Also remember to smile often and to look ahead.

The moon has many faces
crescent face, round face, dark face, bright face
it is not just a mirror of the sun.
The lake has many expressions
violent in a storm, peaceful in calm weather
changing colors, changing character

it is not just a mirror of the sky.
You, me, and the flower
we reflect the Earth, our mother
always adding something new
as we become a son, or a daughter. (J. E.)

ACKNOWLEDGMENTS

I sincerely believe that if you can meditate well, if you can be at peace with your-self, if you can cultivate an open and loving heart, then you've got it made—your life is off to a good start in all its aspects, from work to family to relationships. This book came out that conviction. It was nourished with the stories of people who have been coming to me for meditation training. I thank all those who came in groups and privately for opening up and letting me into their worlds. Without such an intimate knowledge of what needs are out there, this book would never have been written.

Once again, my heartfelt thanks to Thich Nhat Hanh for his support and con-tinued inspiration. His presence, his books, and the videos of his talks on the Plum Village website are a constant source of insight. I thrive on these and recommend them to anyone who feels in need of encouragement and awakening. Knowing him and the Plum Village community, particularly Sister Chân Khong, has been a cherished privilege.

Thanks to Chantal Jacques, who read an early version of this book and made many valuable suggestions. Her intimate knowledge of the subject and experience with meditation make her comments particularly helpful and relevant.

Thanks also to Gabrielle Cloutier and Kirsten Anderson for many inspiring singing sessions. The songs in this book never sounded better than when you sang them.

I owe many thanks to Greg Mulcair for performing small miracles to solve website problems. You will see his work at MindfulnessMeditationCentre.org, where the Guided Meditations and Practice Songs are located.

And thanks to Andrew Yackira, my editor at Tarcher/Penguin for making it all so easy. I have enjoyed your encouraging and friendly way of getting this book ready.